About the Author

An active professional in the investment industry since 1993, Renata Neufeld worked for many years as a financial advisor for an international brokerage firm, managing a significant portfolio of assets for private clients and institutions.

In 2001 she started a boutique investment management firm offering one of the first hedge fund linked notes in Canada. She recently sold the company to start StreetSmarts Omnimedia Corporation.

A native of Montreal, Renata is a graduate of McGill University with a Bachelor of Commerce degree. She is a Certified Investment Manager, Certified Financial Planner, Certified Hedge Fund Specialist, and a Fellow of the Canadian Securities Institute.

Renata has taught the Intelligent Investing Course offered by the Canadian Securities Institute, and is a frequent lecturer and writer on financial issues.

An active participant in philanthropic activities, Renata is donating a portion of the proceeds of this book to Hedge Funds Care, a charity dedicated to the prevention and treatment of child abuse.

She lives in Toronto, Canada.

www.hedgefundlady.com

A special thanks to ...

Steve Kangas, Kangas Consulting
James Wanstall, Abria Financial Group
Dan Hallett, Hallett & Associates
Oliver Schupp, Credit Suisse First Boston
Jason Swales, MacGyver
Scot Blythe, Investments Editor, Advisor.ca
Dan Pembleton, Accilent Capital
Terry Engelman-Rhoadz, Norshield Financial Group
Jeffrey Sarrett, Sandalwood Securities
Bob Thompson, Canaccord Capital
Keith Richards, CIBC Wood Gundy
Tony Porcheron, Raymond James
Tim Martins, RJS Private Wealth Management
Rob D'Angelo, RJS Private Wealth Management
Paul Wylie, ScotiaMcLeod
Gary Ostoich, McMillan Binch
Rob Andrus, National Bank Financial
Darren McKall, Ontario Securities Commission
Ken Stern, Ken Stern Creative Planning Group
Chris Zigrovic, TD Waterhouse Investment Advice
Stanley Rapkin, SF Group
Don MacDonald, Goodman Private Wealth Management
And a very special thanks to my wonderful editor, *Sally Christie.*

ISBN 0-9748354-0-4

Library of Congress Control Number: 2003116162

Published in Canada by Doubletree Press (Canada) Inc.

Disclaimer: A Practical Guide to Hedge Funds contains the opinions and ideas of its author. It is sold with the understanding that the author and publisher are not engaged in the business of rendering investment advice, or legal, accounting, or other professional services. The Guide does not contain legal, accounting, investment or other professional services or advice. The information in the Guide should not be relied upon for any such purpose or purposes. If the reader requires investment advice or legal advice, accounting advice or other professional services, a competent professional should be consulted. The author and publisher therefore disclaim any responsibility for any liability, loss or risk incurred as a consequence of the use or application of any of the contents of this book.

Production Credits:
Cover & Graphic Design: Studiobee
Editor: Victoria White
Photography: Cliff Spicer Photography

Printed in Canada

The Hedge Fund Lady™

A Practical Guide to Hedge Funds

How to profit in
any market

Renata Neufeld, CFP

*"To be a man is, precisely, to be responsible. It is to feel shame
at the sight of what seems to be unmerited misery. It is to take
pride in a victory won by one's comrades. It is to feel, when setting
one's stone, that one is contributing to the building of the world."*
— Antoine de Saint Exupéry, Wind, Sand and Stars

"One of the best ways to make money is not to lose it."
— Old street wisdom

Contents

Introduction

Hedge fund investing is growing at a faster rate than any other kind of investing.

In the last decade, hedge funds have grown from $50 billion in 1993 to approximately $600 billion in 2003. *That's an increase of 1084%.* During that same time frame, the assets in mutual funds increased by 289%. *

There are currently between 6000-7000 hedge funds worldwide, with assets of approximately $600 to $650 billion. Industry predictions are that assets will exceed $1 trillion in the next 5 to 10 years, as individual investors, pension plans, and endowments seek to diversify their holdings.

You probably don't have a lot of extra time on your hands to read about hedge funds. You know there's a lot of information you need to read and to understand about your investments, but you find wading through financial books, quite frankly, boring. You know you should, you know it's important, but it's just so painful sometimes. I understand. Even though I'm in the financial services industry, I too find a lot of the information written in a way that's beyond most people's understanding.

I thought, if I'm going to write about hedge funds, it should be written in a clear, understandable way. I also thought you should be able to read a book about them in a reasonable amount of time because I'm assuming you have a life outside of investing.

This book will not be painful, it might even be mildly pleasant, and I have done my best to present the information in a way that will be interesting and insightful. This book will be useful if you already invest in hedge funds and want to know more, or if you are a complete novice and don't know a thing about them. This book is also a great primer if you're a financial professional wanting to know more about hedge funds to better serve your clients.

So, I've taken all the rocket-science hedge fund material I could get my hands on, read it, analyzed it, thought about it, slept on it, and wrote it down in a short book. This is a book that you can read in a

* SEC Report on Implications of Hedge Fund Growth, Sept.2003, Henessee Group Roundtable discussion

few hours. After you've read it, you'll have a basic understanding of what hedge funds are, how they work, how they compare to mutual funds and other traditional investments, and what the results will likely be if you invest in them.

This is one of the few books where you will also have a chance to read about other people's investment experiences with hedge funds, the good and the bad.

You will also see why, in my humble opinion, hedge funds make sense for a portion of your portfolio.

While once only available to the rich and super rich, hedge funds are now becoming more widely available to the average investor. The more you know, no matter which category you fall into, the better armed you are for creating a positive investment experience.

Enjoy. Learn. Make money. Be wise. Keep it.

Best wishes,

Renata Neufeld

1

What's wrong with investing the way I always have?

---

*"If you always do what you've always done,
you always get what you always got."*
– old proverb

There's a big problem with only going long

Remember "buy & hold"? That's what we've been conditioned to do for a really long time; buy stocks, bonds, mutual funds in our portfolios, and just wait patiently until the market goes up to make money. That's what "going long" is, and chances are good you're already doing it in your portfolio. To go long is simply to hold an investment in your portfolio, whether it's a stock, a bond, or a mutual fund, and make a gain on it when the market goes up. I bet you can see the problem with this already: *the market has to go up for you to make money.*

The bigger problem is that markets go down. I'm sure this comes as no surprise to you. When you hold investments in your portfolio that are long only, which are most traditional investments like stocks, bonds, and mutual funds, they rely on the market going up for you to do well. It's that simple. The market goes up, your mutual fund goes up — the market goes down, your fund goes down. Now, of course that's not a problem when the market goes up, but wouldn't it be nice to have an alternative when things go sideways or down?

The market is a mess

Look at what has happened just since 2000: 9/11, Enron, WorldCom, Tyco, dot.com mania & bust, the S&P plunges by 40%, the on-going investigations of the mutual fund companies, and that's just off the top of my head. Just read the headlines in the daily paper: the market is going up, the market is going down. Oh no, wait — it's back up again. No, spoke too soon — back down.

Hope. Greed. Fear. Plummeting stock prices. Decimated retirement accounts. Shocking corporate scandals. An economic report comes out, the market thinks it's not as positive as it should have been, or what it was expecting it to be, and boom, the Dow Jones Index drops a dramatic 300 points. Or XYZ.com comes out with less of a loss than it should have come out with, and the market sends the stock shooting up 20% in an hour. Welcome to the twenty-first century, folks.

The roaring 1990s of steadily increasing indexes are definitely over. You have to think about investing more now than you ever did. From a high of 5048 on March 10, 2000 (remember when all was good with the world?) the Nasdaq Composite index lost over 2000 points (40%) in a grueling, shocking four weeks. Imagine, you spend years building up your investment account only to lose it in a few months. I'm sure many of you don't have to imagine this scenario because it has actually happened to you. Not many people can afford that and even if you could afford it, who wants to see a substantial part of their portfolio wiped out so quickly?

The Nasdaq went on to lose over 70% of its value in 2000-2001, costing average citizens billions of dollars. Now the Nasdaq is up almost 47% in the 10 months year-to-date from January 2003. How do you prepare for volatility of returns like that? How do you position your portfolio to take advantage of, or mitigate the risks of market movement like that?

We've all met someone, somewhere, who claims they can time the market, buying stocks at just the right time, and selling them just before the market plunges, making a fortune. As an advisor, someone like this would invariably show up to one of my seminars, sit in the first row, and try to prove their brilliance to the room. We hear this and think, "Gee, that doesn't sound so hard. Maybe I'll go out, get some books and do some charts."

The average person (and that's most of us) misses the boat at timing the market. Why? Have you ever listened to a panel of economists? How many conclusions do you get? Even if you had all the time and resources in the world to devote to studying the gyrations and patterns and complexities of the market (and I'm assuming you have other things to do) you'd still probably only be right some of the time. There are money managers, analysts and economists who try to predict the direction of the market *all day, every day.* They're surrounded by some pretty complete data, powerful machines, complex research, and any other tool you can think of to be able to do this kind of analysis. And well, to be blunt, you don't see them floating around on a yacht somewhere. They're still working. If they could predict the markets with any level of accuracy, they wouldn't be there.

Add to this the fact that the market is acting in a way that is more unpredictable today than it ever was, and you can pretty much forget about timing it. I'm not saying some people can't do it some of the time, but nobody can do it all the time, not even the professionals.

So, what do we do? We invest on whims and headlines, instincts and hot tips. We hope. We pray. We focus on the possibilities. Maybe the market will go up this year, we think. Maybe the bear market is really over. "My mutual fund newsletter said the bear market was over!" you exclaim. I know, I've read those rosy reports too. And you know what? Maybe they're right. The S&P 500 Index is up over 24% in the first three quarters of 2003. Maybe our retirement funds will get back to where they were a couple of years ago? Maybe.

The point is this: nobody knows what is going to happen. Nobody. In fact, anything can happen. Just look at what has happened already. Unfortunately, and clearly, we just can't rely on the stability of the market long-term. There is no stability; it's just not there any more. You can't invest like you used to because *your long only investments are tied to that unstable market.*

So what now? Guaranteed investments like government bonds? Well, I recently opened the newspaper to find a big ad for Canada Savings Bonds, paying an average of 3.34% over 5 years. I guess that's not so bad if you think about what the markets have done or what you may have lost in your own portfolio over the last couple of years. Actually, 3.34% sounds pretty good, doesn't it? I bet you wish that you could go back in time and invest all your money in guaranteed investments.

Unfortunately, at 3%, your money would double every 24 years. If you have some losses you'd like to recoup from the market, guaranteed term deposits will take you a very, very long time at the current rates. We wouldn't be having this conversation in the good old days of 8,10,12% interest rates. You could just rush out, invest your money in T-bills or other guaranteed vehicles then go to sleep for 15 years. Ah, how nice that would be!

But at 3%, it's a different story. Subtract from that 3% the effects of inflation and taxes, and you're left with pretty much zero. After you account for inflation, which is currently 2.32% according to InflationData.com, and the taxes you pay on your interest (which is close to 50% for many of us) you're left with close to nothing. If inflation goes up and the rate of interest stays the same, you can actually lose money on a guaranteed investment, which means you might have done better by sticking your money in a mattress. The only one making money is your bank. So, what do you do?

You need to have investments in your portfolio that can pay you a reasonable rate of return but that are not tied to the market like mutual funds and other long only investments. "But I'm diversified in my portfolio" you say. "I have U.S. equities, European mutual funds, and a healthcare fund. I've spread out my risk across different investments."

Let's look at what diversification is for just a second.

To diversify is to reduce your exposure to risk (volatility in your returns) by combining investments in your portfolio that don't all move in the same way, either up or down, at the same time. Have you noticed your portfolio is still down even with all that diversification? Do you know why that may be the case? *Because traditional markets are all highly correlated, which means they all tend to move in the same direction at the same time.* Your U.S. equities, European mutual fund and healthcare fund are all traditional investments, so they will all go up and down at about the same time.

I remember when I was an advisor a few years ago, I would show my clients the famous Ibbotson Chart. Everyone had one in his or her office. It was a chart showing the power of investing in the stock market and how the different geographic markets did at different times.

It was a great argument as to why a client needed to have different types of (long only) investments in their portfolio — so they could diversify properly.

In the good old days of the 90's when everything was going up, you *really could* diversify your portfolio by holding investments from Canada, the U.S. and Europe. You could diversify by holding smaller companies and larger ones, growth stocks and value stocks. But today, all the markets are so inter-related, they're acting very similarly. They tend to go up at the same time, and as you may see from your own portfolio, they go down at the same time too. *There is no true diversification anymore among traditional markets.* Only a guaranteed T-bill and alternative investments are not tied to the market, and we've talked about some of the downfalls of investing in guaranteed investments. An alternative investment would be gold, or real estate, or fine art. It would also be a hedge fund. This book will focus on hedge funds.

2

What is a hedge fund and how is it different from a mutual fund?

People's eyes would glaze over when they asked me what my book was going to be about and I answered, "Hedge funds". Most people don't understand hedge funds and are confused about what they really are, because there is no established definition. I use this analogy to explain what hedge funds are: Two construction workers are working on a house. One worker can only use a hammer, the other worker is given a complete set of tools: nails, screwdriver, saw, hammer — the whole bit. Who is going to do a better job building? Obviously the worker with the whole tool kit. Think of hedge funds as representing the "whole tool kit" that the investment world has to offer. The long only investor, on the other hand, is like the worker with just the hammer. He only has one tool at his disposal, so his house might not be built properly. This brings me to a great quote:

> *"If all you have is a hammer, everything looks like a nail."*
> *– attributed to Baruch's Law*

A hedge fund is a vehicle that does not limit the financial tools that a manager has at his disposal to make a profit. The use of these various tools, which we'll talk about, allows a hedge fund to react to changes in the market in a different way than a traditional long only investment like a mutual fund, where the manager can only buy and hold stocks and bonds.

A hedge fund is really a structure, or category of investing that represents a broad range of different strategies. A hedge fund is like a restaurant. You have fast food restaurants, upscale restaurants, pubs, eateries, and self-serve cafeterias. Then, you can have different kinds within these categories: Italian restaurants, French restaurants, sandwich shops, etc. In this way, they are similar to mutual funds that come in many different shapes and sizes. The categories of mutual funds range from large cap U.S. blue chip to small cap Japanese technology — and everything in between.

Many industry professionals argue (and I agree with them) that because of their different characteristics, hedge funds are a different asset class altogether. An asset class is a separate investment category like equities, bonds, or real estate. Others argue that this is not the case.

Hedge funds play to a different drum than traditional vehicles like equities or mutual funds. They are not limited in going long and as such, have a low or sometimes no correlation to the traditional markets at all. The strategies employed in hedge funds, which we'll talk about a bit later, are much less dependent on the market than regular long only investments like stocks, bonds, and mutual funds. There are certain types of hedge funds that have a higher correlation to the market, but some would argue that this is because they are not truly *hedged.*

To *hedge* is to reduce the risk of a negative price movement in one security or investment by taking an offsetting position in a related security or investment. This is where you might hear the expression "hedging your bets", which implies you protect yourself from the negative outcome of something by taking an offsetting position in something else. Fire insurance is a type of hedge. You don't plan on your house burning down, but you hedge yourself in case it does.

A hedge fund is off in its own world, away from the traditional markets, which is a good thing. If you want to really diversify your portfolio away from traditional investments like stocks or mutual funds, you need to add an investment vehicle that doesn't react the same way to market movements. Hedge funds *have the potential to make money in a down market* because they are often uncorrelated to the traditional markets.

Hedge fund strategies have been garnering a lot of attention recently simply because some of them have had positive performance when all other investments have been negative. In reality, hedge funds have been around since 1949. Unfortunately, nobody really cared about properly diversifying a portfolio when they could make 20% just by getting up in the morning. We may have learned the hard way, but the days of 20% returns with no apparent risk are over.

The main focus of hedge funds is an absolute return objective, the goal being, to make a positive return (i.e. above zero) in any market environment. Losses are not acceptable, regardless of what the overall market has done. When your objective is *to get more than zero,* regardless of what the index does, it changes the whole methodology for getting to your end destination.

Let's do a comparison of some of the differences between hedge funds and mutual funds and then go through them. By the end, I think you'll really start to get a better feel for hedge funds and how they operate.

Mutual Funds	Hedge Funds
1. Aim to outperform a market benchmark like the S&P 500	Aim to get absolute returns regardless of the benchmark
2. Highly correlated to traditional equity/bond markets	Little or no correlation to traditional equity/bond markets
3. Limited in investment strategies	Unlimited in investment strategies
4. Highly regulated, registered with various national securities regulators	Not as regulated, registration not required
5. Small minimum investment	Usually large minimum investment (but not always)
6. Manager is compensated by salary & bonus and/or flat management fee based on assets	Manager compensated primarily on performance incentive
7. Manager doesn't always invest their own capital	Manager almost always invests their own capital
8. Is virtually unlimited in its size	Is usually capped at a maximum size
9. Offered by a prospectus	Offered by an offering/private placement memorandum (OM)
10. Daily liquidity and redemption	Redemption varies from monthly to yearly depending on the fund
11. Is free to advertise to the public	Is restricted in advertising to the public
12. Investment process is clear and usually easy to understand	Investment process is often hard to define and not widely communicated

1. Mutual Funds	Hedge Funds
Aim to outperform a market benchmark like the S&P 500	Aim to get absolute returns regardless of benchmark

A benchmark is a measuring stick by which we measure something. For traditional money managers that benchmark is the index corresponding to their investment mandate. So, for example, a U.S. equity manager who invests in large U.S. companies might have the S&P 500 Index of the largest 500 companies in the U.S. as the benchmark against which to compare his own performance.

If the S&P 500 is down 20% in a year, and your U.S. equity mutual fund is down only 15%, the portfolio manager is ecstatic because they outperformed their benchmark by 5%, and may even get a performance bonus. But you've still lost money.

Do you think about your investments in this way: "Well, I only lost $50,000 instead of $60,000"? Why should you have to lose anything at all? I know why. Because you've been conditioned, as I have, to think there is no other option. We've been conditioned to think this way because for so long, frankly, no other way came to our attention. It was the nature of investing. Period. You invest in the market and it goes up and down, and with any luck, over the long-term, it will go up. Diversify, spread your risk, don't time the market, and you'll be okay over the long-term. This is, of course, simplifying things, but that's pretty much the message you'll get in many existing investment books. It's the way we've been taught for so long by our advisors, by the fund companies, by portfolio managers, by economists, analysts, and investment gurus. It's not that they're misleading us, it's just that you can only do so much with a hammer.

Hedge funds, by contrast, focus on absolute returns, not relative returns. This is probably one of the most important distinctions between hedge funds and mutual funds. Hedge funds focus on getting more than zero and trying never to lose any money, regardless of what the traditional market index does. The benchmark for hedge funds is the thickness of your wallet. If you think about it, how important is anything else in comparison?

2. Mutual Funds	Hedge Funds
Highly correlated to the traditional equity/bond markets	Little or no correlation to traditional equity/bond markets

We spoke about this earlier. In general, there is little or no correlation between hedge funds and what the traditional equity/bond markets are doing. Investing in hedge funds is investing in another asset class altogether. Your hedge fund will "zig" while other investments "zag" and vice-versa. For example, if the market drops by 20% your hedge fund won't likely follow it. It also means that if the market jumps 20% your hedge fund won't likely follow either. You can't have everything. Personally, I would gladly give up a few percentage points on the upside so I don't lose it on the downside.

3. Mutual Funds	Hedge Funds
Limited in investment strategies	Unlimited in investment strategies

Remember the example of building the house with just a hammer, or having a whole tool kit at your disposal? Mutual fund managers frequently have their hands tied behind their back. They are holding only hammers and thus are very limited in their investment strategies. A mutual fund manager is restricted mainly to going long, and not much else. They like the market, they go long. They hate the market, they go long. They can't find any values in the market, they go long. They see a fantastic arbitrage trade in the market, they go long. You get the idea. They just can't do much more than their mandate permits them to do, which is, go long.

This is obviously fine — great even, when the market is rising, but not so great when the market is not. Because of their strict mandates, mutual funds tend to be fully invested in the market at all times, even when they don't want to be. They have strict mandates because it's part of their DNA, so to speak. If, on the other hand, a hedge fund manager doesn't see any value in the market or doesn't see any opportunities to invest in, they can just sit and wait it out in cash.

Hedge funds are far less restricted in their mandates and have many more "tools" in their kit to use in order to make money in the market. We'll talk about these tools in detail later on.

4. Mutual Funds	Hedge Funds
Highly regulated, registered with various national securities regulators	Not as regulated, registration not usually required

Mutual funds are extremely regulated vehicles. Mutual fund companies, as well as the fund managers, are registered, audited, and checked out in great detail by various securities regulators. A mutual fund cannot be offered to the public until the securities regulators have thoroughly reviewed the offering document, the manager and the fund company. They do a background check on the fund manager and the company, investigating their financials, methods of portfolio management, their holdings, which markets they will be investing in, how they will be investing, what clients will be buying, and how they've changed from the last time. Absolutely everything.

Hedge fund managers are not regulated in the same way. They don't have to register with regulators, although the SEC has proposed that they do. (In Canada they currently do.) Consequently, hedge fund managers are construed as somewhat of a secretive bunch. Why don't they have to register? In general, to offer any kind of security for sale to the public you can do one of two things: (1) you can register yourself and your company with the appropriate securities regulators or (2) you can avoid registering by relying on an exclusion or exemption. This exclusion will apply if you meet certain criteria, such as having a limited number of investors, all of whom have to meet certain minimum income or minimum investment tests.

So, if the hedge fund doesn't want to offer its securities to the general public, just to a limited group of high net worth investors, they can be excluded from registration. Because they don't have to register with the securities regulators, they don't have to report their holdings. They don't even have to be audited, although more and more are going that route to help investors become comfortable with them and dispel some of the mystery. I'm simplifying it here, but we'll come back to the registration issue again.

What does the regulation issue mean for you? Well, in theory, something that is more regulated and more "policed" is safer to invest in. Having something that is highly regulated should help eliminate incidents of fraud. As you may have read in the papers recently, there are several big name U.S. mutual fund companies under investigation. Clearly, there is no guarantee, even with strict regulation that there won't be fraud or mismanagement.

So, does the lack of regulation of hedge funds compared to mutual funds make them more dangerous? Potentially, yes, if you don't do your homework. Doing your homework is asking some very detailed questions of the fund manager and their operations which we'll talk about in greater detail in our chapter, due diligence. Because there is no national body regulating hedge funds, the responsibility of researching them and keeping on top of them ultimately falls to you, my friend. "That's a lot of work!" you exclaim, and you're right. Are there ways you can manage or even mitigate some of this risk? Absolutely, and we'll talk about them.

5. Mutual Funds	Hedge Funds
Small minimum investment	Usually large minimum investment (but not always)

Mutual funds are available to just about anybody who wants to invest in them. You can walk into any bank, almost anywhere, and they'll sell you a mutual fund. Hedge funds, on the other hand, because of their loosely regulated environment, are only available to investors who are "accredited investors". As an accredited investor you must meet the following criteria:

- You have a minimum net worth of $1 million alone or with your spouse or,
- You have made an income of $200,000 in the last 2 years and expect to make that going forward or,
- You and your spouse make a combined income of $300,000 and expect to make that going forward.
- If you are a corporation, a partnership, or anything other than a person, you have to have a minimum net worth of $5,000,000.
- In Canada, you can forego the first four rules if you have a minimum of $150,000 to invest into a hedge fund. (This applies to most provinces in Canada.) In Canada, you must have $1 million of net liquid assets, not including your home or other securities.

For more specific information on what is considered an accredited investor, please visit the securities commission website corresponding to where you live.

If you meet any of these criteria, the investment minimum in a hedge fund is set according to the specific manager. This is based on the notion that if you meet a certain minimum investment criteria, you can afford to take on the risk associated with investing in hedge funds.

For those reading this who don't meet those criteria and wonder if they should continue reading, the answer is yes. There are a number of different product structures that allow you access to hedge funds for much lower minimums. They warrant a whole chapter in the book, so read on.

6. Mutual Funds	Hedge Funds
Manager is compensated by salary & bonus and/or flat management fee based on assets	Manager is compensated primarily on performance incentive

There is a fundamental difference in the way mutual fund managers get paid and the way hedge fund managers get paid. This difference is what I call a "put your money where your mouth is" difference. A mutual fund manager will typically collect a salary and a bonus. The bonus will be based to a large degree on the management fee that the fund collects. The more money that goes into the fund, the higher the management fee, and the more the mutual fund manager receives. If the fund does well and grows by increasing its performance, it also gets to collect a higher fee; it's a straight percentage on the amount of assets. The more assets the better.

The problem with this model is that when the fund has mediocre performance, or loses money, the mutual fund manager still collects a fee. Granted, it's a fee on a slightly smaller pool of assets if the fund has gone down in value, but the fee percentage still doesn't change. A fund manager will never come to you and say, "You know what Joe, I feel just terrible we didn't make any money this quarter. Don't worry about it, you don't have to pay me." Regardless of the performance of the mutual fund, the compensation structure remains the same. So you just have to hope for a sunny day.

A hedge fund manager still receives a general management fee for the assets under management, but that fee is often lower than a mutual fund fee. Hedge fund managers make the majority of their income based on their performance. If the fund does well, they do well. If the fund doesn't do well, they don't either. Hedge fund managers' compensation is directly tied to their performance.

Now, I won't tell you these performance fees are inexpensive, because they're not. A typical example of a performance fee would be 20%. Remember that's 20% of your profits. If there are no profits, there is no performance fee. If you're paying a large performance fee, it's because you've made a large return. Of course, to some people fees are always an issue no matter what the return.

A manager will often only charge a performance fee over some kind of "hurdle rate". A hurdle rate is the minimum rate of return the manager must earn before they can charge you a performance fee. This changes depending on the manager but they can't charge you a performance fee unless they get above zero. Many managers will use the T-bill rate while some managers who want to attract more clients will choose a higher threshold.

Here's how the performance fees would work: if you invested $100,000 with manager Peggy Sue and she makes you 10% one year (before fees are subtracted) her fee may be "1&20 with a T-bill hurdle rate". That means Peggy Sue will charge you a 1% flat fee on the amount you invest with her and 20% of all profits she makes over the T-bill rate. So, if the T-bill rate is 3%:

Management Fee: $100,000 * 1% = $1000 flat fee
Performance Fee: 20% of 7% (7% is the return she got you over her hurdle 10%-3%) = 1.4%
so another $1400 in a performance fee.
Total fees are $1000+$1400= $2400 (or 2.4%).

Another piece to the performance puzzle is something called a "high-water mark". If a fund has this, it means that performance fees aren't charged until the fund's performance has surpassed its previous highest performance. What this means for you is that if your hedge fund goes up 10% then drops 5% and goes up by 3%, *you won't pay a performance fee until the performance surpasses the previous*

10% it made for you; you won't have to pay a fee until they make up those losses. You'll pay a performance fee for the 10%, no fee for it going down 5%, and no fee on new the 3%. (After going down 5%.) If the fund went up 6% instead of 3% you would be at an 11% return, but you would only pay a performance fee on the 1% difference between 11% and your "high water mark" of 10%. Make sure the fund has a high-water mark. Most do.

7. Mutual Funds	Hedge Funds
Manager doesn't always invest own capital	Manager almost always invests own capital

This is another "put your money where your mouth is" point. A mutual fund manager will not always invest his or her own investment funds into their fund. Why? No, not because there are legal restrictions preventing it, but because they often find their own mandates too restrictive. What if the mutual fund manager didn't like the market, hated it in fact, but the mandate of his fund was to be fully invested at all times, no moving to bonds or cash? Nor could he use any other investment techniques to mitigate some of the losses if the market drops. Oh, and he was also limited to small-cap technology stocks.

It's not that the mutual fund manager doesn't have faith in his own stock picks or abilities, it's just that the mandate of his fund (and mutual funds in general) is just far too restrictive. If a mutual fund manager has a different view of the market, why would he invest in his own fund if it forces him to be long only with no room to maneuver? A hedge fund manager almost always invests a significant portion of his own money in his own fund. Why wouldn't he if he felt he had all the tools at his disposal to make money?

Hedge fund managers are more "entrepreneurial" than mutual fund managers are. Typically, they are not hired to manage a fund as a mutual fund manager would be hired. Many of them usually start their own fund after establishing a track record in traditional investment management. They attract funds from other private investors who may know them personally and know of their track record.

If you think about it logically, why would anyone want to have his or her money managed by someone who isn't managing his own money in the exact same way? This is definitely a plus. How much more aligned could a manger be to your own interest than by having his funds in beside yours? You can bet he'll be doing his best to perform better and manage risk better because his investment is at risk too.

8. Mutual Funds	Hedge Funds
Are virtually unlimited in their size	Are usually capped at a maximum size

Very few mutual funds are capped or closed off to new investors, unless they have a specialized strategy that can only handle so much cash coming in before they run out of investment opportunities. Most mutual funds are always open for business. The more assets they have under management, the more fees they can collect.

This can have a downside, as you may know. Sometimes, when a fund (and this can be a mutual fund or a hedge fund as the same applies to both) is bogged down with too much cash, it's hard to make investments in the market that will affect the portfolio, so the returns get diluted.

For example, if a mutual fund (and you see this all the time) has excellent performance, everyone wants to invest in it. So, there is a huge inflow of cash from investors wanting that dazzling return. If the fund is, for example, a $50 million fund, and all of a sudden $20 million comes in the door, the size of the fund jumps dramatically. Whatever good investments the fund manager may make has to be spread over a bigger pie so the effect of his performance will be much lower, at least until he can invest all the cash and put it to work.

Another thing that can happen is that the mutual fund gets so big it actually moves markets when it buys or sells stocks. That means when a $2 billion fund, which is very common, has a 5% position in a stock, that's a $100 million investment in a company. If the fund manager doesn't like that stock and wants to sell it, the price will likely be pushed down because $100 million worth of one stock is being sold.

The last thing a hedge fund manager wants to do is jeopardize his returns because that's where his bread is really buttered, thanks to performance fees. In the hedge fund world, smaller is better, because bigger may mean lower performance and therefore less fees. In fact, performance matters to them so much that hedge fund managers will often cap their funds before they get too big so as not to endanger their performance.

9. Mutual Funds	Hedge Funds
Offered by a prospectus	Offered by an offering/private placement memorandum (OM)

What's the difference between an offering/private placement memorandum and a prospectus? A prospectus is a comprehensive legal document that is filed and reviewed by the securities regulators. A prospectus is the legal "offering document" that the mutual fund will issue to inform potential investors about the fund. It will outline such things as the fund's investment strategy, for whom it's intended, what the risks are, what the fees are, and how you can buy it.

Most hedge funds are offered by an offering memorandum. An offering/private placement memorandum is usually shorter and comes with a subscription agreement. A subscription agreement is a document the investor signs saying he understands the risks associated with the investment, and that he's an accredited investor. There's also another kind of legal offering document called an information statement that we'll talk about in chapter 9.

The prospectus must be approved by the securities regulators before the fund can be made available for sale; there's that extra level of "protection". This goes back to the regulation issue we spoke about earlier. There's the knowledge that authorities are looking through it with a fine-tooth comb before they will allow it to be offered to the public. It's not a guarantee of performance, of course, but at least you know your i's are dotted and the t's are crossed.

An offering/private placement memorandum doesn't need to be filed with the securities regulators, so you're on your own to make sure everything is where it should be. If you invest in mutual funds yet haven't read a prospectus, then you're like most people — it arrives in the mail and often goes to the recycling bin. If you're going to buy a hedge fund on the other hand, I would strongly urge you to read the offering/private placement memorandum. Make notes on what you don't understand, then ask the manager or your planner/advisor about it until you feel comfortable. You need to do your homework here. In the case of the hedge funds, you are the one who's dotting the i's and crossing the t's.

10. Mutual Funds	Hedge Funds
Offer daily liquidity and redemption	Redemption varies from monthly to yearly depending on the fund

You can sell your mutual fund the next day but not sell your hedge fund for one month or more. That has to do with the often-illiquid nature of the investments in the hedge fund portfolio. Liquidity means you can sell an investment in a day and turn it into cash. A T-bill is liquid; a large U.S company stock is liquid. When something is liquid, it is because there is an instant market for it; you can sell it almost immediately. An example of something that is *illiquid* would be real estate. You probably couldn't sell your house the very next day and collect a cheque. Even if you could sell it in a day, you'd have to collect the funds from the buyer and do all the paperwork, etc. As we'll see later on when we discuss the various strategies, some of the investments that the hedge fund manager invests in are *illiquid;* she might not be able to get out of them quickly, particularly if they are complex trades.

You may be apprehensive and think, "I don't want to tie my money up. I want to have access to it whenever I want it." Here's a really important point that people don't realize when they think about liquidity, and Alexander M. Ineichen, in his book, *"Absolute Returns"* said it perfectly: "Liquidity is correlated with efficiency. The more efficient a market, the higher the liquidity. High liquidity and high efficiency mean close to perfect information and competition. Perfect information and perfect competition mean fewer opportunities to exploit inefficiencies."

What he is saying is that if an investment strategy is really liquid and efficient, you generally can't make any money in it because everyone is doing the same thing. T-bill markets, for example, are very liquid and efficient. Remember, you make money by exploiting inefficiencies in the market. Hedge funds are much better positioned to exploit these inefficiencies than traditional long only vehicles.

11. Mutual Funds	Hedge Funds
Are free to advertise to the public	Are restricted in advertising to the public

You see mutual fund investments advertised in the newspaper all the time. Mutual fund companies spend millions of dollars on advertising every year. In contrast, because of the less regulated environment of hedge funds, the regulators won't let them advertise. (In Canada this is not the case; they are allowed to advertise.) This adds to the whole "mystery" surrounding hedge funds. We never hear a thing about them, until there's an uncommon blow-up. When we hear about it in the news, it makes it seem like all hedge fund managers are large risk takers, or corrupt in some way, and that's simply not the case. You never hear about 99.9% of hedge fund managers who just quietly go about doing their business.

This may change in the future. One of the recommendations of the September 2003 SEC Report entitled "Implications of the Growth of Hedge Funds", is to consider allowing hedge funds to advertise under certain circumstances.

12. Mutual Funds	Hedge Funds
Investment process is clear and usually easy to understand	Investment process is often hard to define and not widely communicated

Mutual funds have a pretty easy process to understand. They may buy different kinds of companies in different markets, but basically, they go long. Hedge funds, on the other hand, can have fairly complex trades in complex markets. In general, the strategies that hedge funds use are just harder to describe. In addition to that, when you invest in a mutual fund, you know the fund's objectives and methodologies. You've likely seen a listing of the fund's holdings, you've read about them in the paper, and seen their returns advertised. Mutual funds are very transparent because they adhere to strict regulations .

Because hedge fund managers are not legally obligated to reveal their holdings, they often don't. This can make investors wary because you don't always know what you're investing in, and you have to trust that the manager knows what he's doing. A hedge fund is not an open book like a mutual fund and this can be a real issue for some people. We'll tackle this one later on.

3

More differences: Short-selling, leverage and more

There are a two more important differences between hedge funds and mutual funds that you need to know before you can understand the actual strategies hedge funds use: short-selling and leverage.

Short-selling and leverage can be frightening words to some people. They almost say, "Danger, stay away!" However, as you will see, these somewhat "offensive" strategies are actually used to lower the volatility (and the risk) in your portfolio with hedge funds. You may still think they're dangerous, but if you understood that something was being used as a tool to actually reduce the volatility in your portfolio, wouldn't that make you think twice about it, or at least examine it further?

What is short-selling exactly?

Short-selling is similar to the opposite of going long. When you go long, you make a profit when the stock you have invested in rises. In short-selling you make a profit from the fall of a stock. You borrow a stock for the purpose of selling it to someone else, on the hope of repurchasing it later at a lower price. Financial institutions have arrangements to be able to borrow stocks from each other for the purpose of short-selling. One institution will lend another stock in exchange for a fee, usually the overnight T-bill rate. Short-selling uses the fundamental principle "buy low, sell high", but in the opposite order you're used to.

Let me use a story to explain how it works; Dr. Slimbody has just come out with a new diet book entitled, "Eat Everything You Can and Lose 20 Lbs". This book retails in the store for $30, which you think is absolutely ridiculous. You think this crazy diet book is a big fad and can't believe how popular it has become. The book is so popular it's flying off the shelves. In fact, book stores have run out. People are prepared to pay $40, even $50 a book because there just aren't any left in the bookstores. So people try to buy it on the internet. You, on the other hand, think the price will drop well below the original $30 in a couple of months once people find out this diet doesn't work and that it will be replaced by another fad diet book.

Since your friend has just purchased one of these books for $50, you ask her if you can borrow it from her for the next month or so. As repayment, you will buy her a new pair of leg warmers. She agrees, and lends you the book. The next day, you strategically place yourself in front of a donut shop and sell the book for $50. (You've just sold the book your friend lent you, but it's okay, you'll see.) The buyer thinks this is a pretty good deal, because they can't even get the book for $50 now as the price on the internet has jumped to $60. They eat their donut happily.

Over the next month, your prediction comes true. People all over North America who tried the diet put on an average of 10 pounds, and want to dump their books for the latest diet book:"Eat Pasta & Win". Dr. Slimbody's books are now selling for $10, and there's plenty of them.

So you take your $50 from the original sale of the book, buy the book for the reduced price of $10, then you buy your friend the legwarmers you promised her for $5. You go to your friend's house with the items, thank her for the loan, and go home with $35 in your pocket. This is a short sale.

In short-selling, you borrow a stock from a financial institution that has it. They charge you interest to borrow it (the legwarmers). Once you have it, you can sell it to someone else and pocket the funds from the sale. You would then buy it back at a cheaper price to repay the person — financial institution — you borrowed it from in the first place. The part I left out was that you can also make interest on the cash you get from the short sale since the money makes interest before you use it to buy the stock back at a cheaper price.

The problem with short-selling is, of course, if the price of the stock goes up instead of down, you're in a bit of trouble. If this happens, you have to buy the stock back at a more expensive price than what you sold it for. That can be painful. Technically, the losses are unlimited. If the diet book actually took off and started selling for $100, you've just sold it for $50 and you still owe your friend the book.

If you just "shorted" without anything on the other side to balance you out (like a long position) it can be pretty dangerous. You can protect your downside losses on short sales by setting "stop-loss" provisions in the portfolio. (i.e. If the shares rise above a certain point, you are forced to buy back the shares to cover your short.) Diversification of positions is of course another way to mitigate some of the risks involved with short-selling.

In the context of hedge funds, short-selling is used to "hedge" your bets, to cover yourself if the market goes the other way. Short-selling can actually lower portfolio risk because short positions can reduce your actual exposure to the market. As we've talked about before, if you reduce your exposure to the market, your market risk is reduced, so therefore, you lower your overall portfolio risk.

Leverage: another scary word that's really not so scary

To leverage is to borrow money for the purpose of enhancing your return on a particular investment. It's actually quite common and you're probably using leverage right now without even knowing it. If you own a house, you're probably using leverage. You likely put some money down and borrowed the rest from the bank to buy your property. If you're like most people, you put down 20% of your own money when buying the house and borrowed 80% from the bank. In this case, you are "levered" 4 to 1. Let's use another story to illustrate.

Let's say you sell bait for a living. The better the fishing season, the happier you are. You can sell your bait to the local fishing store for $1 for each unit. You buy your bait from the little kid down the street for $0.50. That's not a bad little business, with a 100% mark-up.

However, you only have $50 to buy this bait because you've just lost all your money in the market. With your $50, you can buy 100 units of bait from the kid down the street, sell them to the fishing store for $1 each and you've made $100 - $50 of profit, and your original investment of $50.

But fishing season is getting into high gear, and if you can buy more bait, you'd make a lot more money. So you go to your local bank and borrow $150 to buy bait, and they charge you $10 interest. Now you've got $200 total to buy bait with (your original $50 and the bank's $150) so you can buy 400 units of bait.

You sell them for $1 each and you've made $390 on your original $50: $400 in sales less the $10 of interest you have to pay the bank. This of course works well if you can sell all your bait as planned. If you can't, that's where things get a little tricky.

Imagine there is a sudden hurricane, which destroys the fishing season. You paid $0.50 to buy each unit of bait, but instead of being able to sell them for $1 as you anticipated, you can only sell them to the store for $0.25. In this case, not only did you lose money but you owe the bank their money too. (And the little kid down the street is a shrewd businessman and won't take the bait back.)

Not every hedge fund uses leverage, and of the ones that do, they don't necessarily use a large amount of it. To me, using some leverage on a highly diversified portfolio is less risky than taking big bets with an un-diversified, un-leveraged portfolio.

This is a perfect time for me to tell you about Alfred Winslow Jones, the creator of the first hedge fund. Mr. Jones was the first one to use what were previously two risky concepts, short-selling and leverage, to actually reduce risk in a portfolio. He did this way back in 1949. We'll go through what he did and how he did it, and then you'll really understand how these tools can be used to reduce the risk in a portfolio. I'll explain, but first let me tell you about Jones.

The Jones that no one kept up with, until they did: A brief history of hedge funds

In 1949, Alfred Winslow Jones started the first hedge fund. The idea came to him when he was doing research for an article he was writing for Fortune magazine where he was an editor. The article was entitled, "Fashions in Forecasting" and he was amazed at the fact that every analyst he interviewed said it was impossible to predict the market's direction.

So Jones set out to create a strategy that was "independent" of the market, and he did. He took old tools like short-selling and leverage, and combined them to get a fundamentally conservative result that could produce returns in both up and down markets. He said he was "using speculative techniques for conservative ends".

Jones lived and worked (he was actually a PhD in sociology) and produced some spectacular results with his fund over the next 17 years. His success was virtually undetected by the media and the general public. Then one day a financial reporter named Carol Loomis wrote an article about Jones entitled, "The Jones Nobody Keeps Up With". Loomis had discovered that Jones had outperformed the best performing mutual fund of the previous 5 years (the Fidelity Trend Fund) by 44%. In the 10 years before that, Jones had outperformed the best mutual fund for that period (the Dreyfus Fund) by 87%.

Investors and fund managers sat up and took notice of Jones, and soon everyone was trying to keep up with him. Two years later there were 200 hedge funds in existence.

Jones did a couple of important things differently in the management of his fund, compared to a traditional long-only mutual fund manager: (1) He invested all his own money in it. (2) He paid himself and his associates on the performance of the fund.

So how did Jones use these two things like short-selling and leverage for conservative means? He used these two techniques to hedge himself against the swings of the market, so regardless of what the market did, he would still make money.

Here was his basic premise: You start out with $100 to invest in the market. You borrow another $20 to invest in the market. Therefore, you have $120 to invest in the market. You buy shares of Vladimir Vodka Co. because you think people are drinking more alcohol and anticipate the shares will climb in value. However, just in case people don't drink more, you sell short $50 of Best Cellars Wines. So, while you're really invested $170 (long position $120 + short position $50) your actual exposure to the market is $70, or 70%. Remember, market exposure means the amount of risk you are taking on by being invested in the market. The more exposure you have to the market, the more your portfolio will fluctuate in accordance with the market:

$$\text{Market exposure} = \frac{\text{long position} - \text{short position}}{\text{original capital}}$$

$$\text{so,} \quad \frac{\$120 - \$50}{\$100} = 70\%$$

Let's compare that with another case. Imagine you really felt confident that people would be drinking more alcohol. You've watched the news; people are more stressed then they've ever been and there are more bars opening in your neighborhood. You want to buy Vladimir Vodka and hold it long. You don't feel the need to short Best Cellars Wines. You also don't want to use leverage. You're just holding a stock on the hope that it will rise in value, like many people do. Here's what your market exposure will look like:

$$\text{Market exposure} = \frac{\text{long position} - \text{short position}}{\text{original capital}}$$

$$\text{so,} \quad \frac{\$100 - \$0}{\$100} = 100\%$$

By combining short-selling and leverage, Jones managed to *diversify away from the market,* which was his goal in the first place (and may be yours by now). By doing so, his strategy became less correlated to the market. Remember, the less exposure you have to the market, the less your investment strategy will move with the market, the more it will move *independently* of the market. So, if you're only 70% exposed versus 100% exposed to the market and the market goes down 10%, your strategy will only go down 7%. The same will happen on the upside. To think, a PhD in sociology came up with that!

The performance of hedge funds

Now that we've seen and covered some of the major differences between hedge funds and traditional equity market or mutual fund investments, let's see how hedge funds as a group have actually done compared to traditional markets like the S&P 500 or the MSCI World Index. (The MSCI World is the largest global index that measures the performance of the markets in North America, Europe, Japan and Asia.)

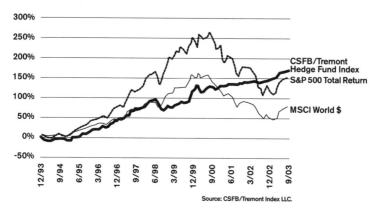

Source: CSFB/Tremont Index LLC.

This chart measures the rate of return of the CSFB/Tremont Hedge Index over the past ten years compared to the "traditional" indexes. $1000 invested in the CSFB/Tremont at the beginning of 1994 would be worth $2746.10 at Sept. 30, 2003. $1000 invested in the S&P 500 Index would be worth $2546.20, and $1000 invested in the MSCI World Index would be worth $1815.90.

Net Performance	CSFB/Tremont Hedge Index	S&P 500 Total Return	MSCI World $
1 Month	1.52%	-1.06%	0.63%
3 Months	2.37%	2.65%	4.94%
6 Months	8.10%	18.45%	23.04%
1 Year	12.85%	24.40%	26.02%
2 Years	16.36%	-1.09%	2.25%
3 Years	18.85%	-27.42%	-26.25%
3yr Avg	**5.93%**	**-10.13%**	**-9.65%**
5 years	53.33%	5.08%	3.94%
5yr Avg	**8.92%**	**1.00%**	**0.78%**
Since Inception	174.61%	154.62%	81.59%
Incep Avg Annl	**10.92%**	**10.06%**	**6.31%**

Source: CSFB/Tremont Index LLC. Data as of September, 2003. Performance data is net of all fees. Index data begins January 1994. Sharpe ratio calculated using a rolling 90-day T-bill rate.

Here are the year-over-year returns:

Year	CSFB/Tremont Hedge Index	S&P 500 Total Return	MSCI World $
2003	10.50%	14.72%	16.96%
2002	3.04%	-22.10%	-19.54%
2001	4.42%	-11.89%	-16.52%
2000	4.85%	-9.10%	-12.92%
1999	23.43%	21.04%	25.34%
1998	-0.36%	28.58%	24.80%
1997	25.94%	33.36%	16.23%
1996	22.22%	22.96%	14.00%
1995	21.69%	37.58%	21.32%
1994	-4.36%	1.32%	5.58%

Source: CSFB/Tremont Index LLC. Data as of September, 2003. Performance data is net of all fees. Index data begins January 1994. Sharpe ratio calculated using a rolling 90-day T-bill rate.

A note about investment returns: Investment returns are usually presented in one of two ways: compounded return, or year-over-year returns. A compound return is the average of the yearly returns. So, if you have a 5-year, annual compound return of 12% that means on average, you received 12% a year over those five years. But what it doesn't tell you is if you lost money in one of those years. Only the annual return or year-over-year numbers will tell you that. Whenever you invest in anything, it's a good idea to see the year-over-year numbers in addition to the average compound return numbers. The year-over-year figures will show you if the fund or investment vehicle has lost money in a year. If you can't handle losing money in a year, you probably shouldn't look at that particular vehicle. In summary, year-over-year just gives you a more complete picture of the returns, and lets you see if there have been negative years that have been "covered up" by really good years.

A note about taxes: *While taxes are important, this book will not discuss the tax consequences of investing in hedge funds. Hedge funds are different from other types of investments you may have previously invested in before and have different tax consequences depending on the specific strategy, and where you live. Please consult a tax professional to discuss your own personal circumstances.*

You may be thinking, "That's great, but isn't it too late now? Haven't I missed the boat? Isn't it too late to get in now? These hedge funds have done so well already." The answer to that is no. Hedge funds are not like traditional market vehicles, so the notions of "overheating", "overvalued", "peaking", and "too late" simply don't apply. Many of the rules that apply to traditional investing just don't apply to hedge funds. Because hedge funds can offset long investments by hedging, things like overvaluation are not a part of the same universe. Now, that being said, there is a downside.

The downside is, if the market goes up tomorrow (as it did in 2003) you may not do as well as your friends who are invested in long only investments. For some people that's a double-edged sword. For others, it's a big sigh of relief.

I'm sure you've heard this before, but you can't have it all. I wish I could tell you with hedge funds you can have it all, but you can't. Hedge funds will, in general, reduce your exposure to the traditional equity markets. If the market goes up dramatically, you probably won't do as well as if you were fully invested in the market.

Don't lose it!

A really important concept I want to discuss is the concept of "wealth preservation". Everybody talks about "preserving your wealth". You see mutual fund or portfolio management brochures talking about this concept all the time. Beautiful, picturesque brochures with gold-embossed font, green trees, and maybe some images of strong, architectural pillars. They all talk about the same thing, about preserving your wealth, and how important it is. It's not about the returns, they say, it's about preservation of capital.

But how will a traditional manager preserve your wealth when the market drops and he has to be fully invested as part of his mandate? It's not impossible I suppose, but very tricky.

> *"The first rule of investment is don't lose. And the second rule of investment is don't forget the first rule. And that's all the rules there are." – Benjamin Graham*

The point about preservation of capital (otherwise known as not losing money) is a valid one. It is important because once you lose money, it's a lot harder to get it back than if you had never lost it in the first place. It's mathematical. Look at this:

Mary starts off with $100,000 in her portfolio:
Here's what happens to her:
Year 1: she's up 15% to $115,000
Year 2: she's up another 15% to $132,250 (compounding effect, it's 15% on more money)
Year 3: up again 15% to $152,087 (lucky Mary)

Bill starts off with $100,000 but has a rockier ride:
Year 1: he's up 15% to $115,000
Year 2: he's down 15% to $97,750
(you see when you lose 15%, you're actually down further than your original investment, even though you were up 15% before)
Year 3: Bill now needs a return of 55% to get to Mary's $152,087. Bill asks Mary to marry him.

55% is a sizeable return Bill has to make up in Year 3. Even if we changed these numbers to 8% or 10%, it's the same principle: when you lose x% you need more than x% to get back to break even. So don't lose money. Simple, isn't it?

It's great to get dazzling returns, but if you have to give it all back, (and as history has shown us you often have to with traditional investments) then you're in a worse spot than you were to begin with.

It's all about the Sharpe Ratio

The Sharpe ratio was named after Professor William F. Sharpe. Professor Sharpe was one of three people who received the Nobel Prize for Economics in 1990, so he's up there on the "rocket-scientist" scale.

The Sharpe ratio is a measure that calculates the risk-adjusted return of an investment. That means this ratio calculates the excess return of something (a portfolio, an index) over the risk-free rate (generally T-bills) and divides it by the risk you need to take on to get that return. The risk-free rate is the rate anybody can get just by getting up in the morning. As the name implies, there is no risk involved in getting this return. The risk you need to take on to get that return is defined as the annualized standard deviation of returns.

Annualized standard deviation of returns shows you the amount the returns can deviate from the usual annual return the investment seems to get. This "usual" return is also called the mean or average return. When you talk about the volatility of an investment, you are talking about the standard deviation of returns.

Volatility is found by calculating the annualized standard deviation of the monthly change in the price of something (a stock, a mutual fund, a hedge fund). If the price of something moves up and down rapidly over short time periods, it has high volatility. If the price almost never changes, it has low volatility. If something has a 30% volatility, it can move 30% in either direction. For example, you can have a 10% return, and with 30% volatility you can have returns anywhere from + 40% to -20% . Let's look at some Sharpe ratios:

Sharpe Ratio: $\dfrac{\text{Return of Fund - Risk-Free Rate (T-bills)}}{\text{Annualized Standard Deviation of Returns}}$

Sharpe Ratio: $\dfrac{20\% - 3\%}{30\%} = 0.90$

What does this number mean? What if you could get the same 20%, but the volatility of your returns was much less, maybe 15% instead of 30%. Then your Sharpe ratio would be:

$$\frac{20\% - 3\%}{15\%} = 1.13$$

In the second example, your annualized standard deviation of returns has gone down substantially from 30% to 15% and your Sharpe ratio has gone up. The higher the Sharpe ratio, the better. Why? Because it means you're taking on less risk per unit of return or, you're getting more return for the same level of risk.

It's a matter of proportion. If your return was 10% but your volatility was only 5% then your Sharpe ratio would be:

$$\frac{10\% - 3\%}{5\%} = 1.4 \text{ , which is even better than 1.13.}$$

Let's put this Sharpe Ratio into the context of the real world. What are the Sharpe Ratios of hedge funds versus traditional indexes?

Strategy	Sharpe Ratio
CSFB/Tremont Hedge Fund Index	0.78
S&P 500 Total Return Index	0.37
MSCI World Index	0.14
Risk Free Rate (T-bill)	0

Source: CSFB/Tremont Index LLC. Sharpe ratio calculated using a rolling 90-Day T-bill rate.

What the Sharpe ratio of your investment tells you is how much "value" your investment has compared to other types of investments. The Sharpe Ratio is kind of like a measure of where all these investments finished in their class at school. If you were an employer interviewing students for a job, wouldn't you want the student with the best marks?

Measuring returns is easy. The Sharpe ratio measures how much pain you have to suffer to get that return. This becomes a meaningful lesson as you get beaten up by the markets time and time again.

Like anything, this measure isn't perfect. Many scientists and industry professionals will argue it's not accurate enough. There are other, more sophisticated, more complicated ratios (all named after the people who invented them) that can measure in greater detail the extent and accuracy of the risk/return ratio. The Sharpe ratio is the most common, most widely used, and available to the public without having to do hours of calculations in a mathematical lab.

Although not perfect, the Sharpe ratio gives you a pretty good picture of the risk-adjusted rate of return of an investment.

So what do you think when you see the Hedge Fund Index Sharpe ratios compared to the traditional indexes? What do these numbers tell you? On a risk-adjusted basis, it seems to me you're better off with hedge funds than you would be by being invested in the S&P 500, or the MSCI World Index, or certainly T-bills. That's a bold statement, isn't it?

That doesn't mean I'm telling you to go out and sell everything you have right now and put it into hedge funds. What I am saying is that if you want to reduce the overall volatility in your portfolio, but still want to be able to generate a return above T-bills, you can do that with hedge funds.

The famous risk/return chart

Ideally, you want the most return, with the least amount of risk. A high return, low risk investment is like "investing nirvana". If T-bills, a "riskless" investment, were paying you 15% would you bother investing in anything else? I wouldn't. I would go to my local bank, invest as much money as I could, then go home and take a nice long 20-year nap.

But, unfortunately, that's not the case. The reality is, you have to invest in something other than a vehicle that yields 3% (and 0% after inflation and taxes) if you want to make any money, or even keep the money you have. What you're trying to accomplish in your portfolio is always getting to the upper left hand side of this risk return chart, the most return for the least amount of risk.

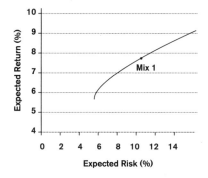

Asset Class	Mix 1
Large Cap	45%
Intl Equity	15%
US Bonds	40%
Expected Return	7.85
Standard Deviation	9.24
Sharpe ratio	0.42

Source: Credit Suisse Asset Management

Adding hedge funds to your portfolio helps you get there.

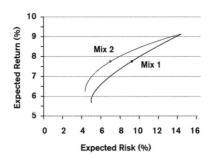

Asset Class	Mix 1	Mix 2
Large Cap	45%	18%
Intl Equity	15%	15%
US Bonds	40%	0%
Hedge Funds	0%	67%
Expected Return	7.85	7.85
Standard Deviation	9.24	7.62
Sharpe Ratio	0.42	0.51

Source: Credit Suisse Asset Management

Alphas & Betas

The next time you're at a party and anyone brings up any type of investment at all, just ask him or her what the alpha is on the strategy. Then hand them an hors d'oeuvre to ease their silence and tell them all you know.

Let's start with beta first; beta is the market, and the risk associated with the market. Pretty simple. To be even more accurate, beta is the measure of the investment strategy's return in relation to the market. For example, if the beta of your fund is 1.0, your fund is perfectly correlated with the market. If the market moves up 9.3% your fund will move up 9.3%.

A beta of greater than 1 means your investment will move more than one-for-one with the market. A beta of greater than 1 means you have a strategy that is more volatile than the market, on the upside, and on the downside. So, if the beta of your strategy is 1.5 and the market goes down 10%, your strategy will go down 1.5 times that, or 15%. A beta of 0.5, and your strategy will move half as much as the market moves. A beta of less than one means your strategy is less volatile than the market, on the upside, and on the downside.

Why is this important? Well, ideally, if you're adding hedge funds to your portfolio to diversify your portfolio away from the market, you want to add in hedge funds that have a beta of less than 1.0 or even zero if you can, so that your portfolio doesn't dance to the market's every move. But, aren't hedge funds supposed to be uncorrelated to the market? You are right; in general, they have a low correlation to the market, or a low beta. There are specific hedge fund strategies, however, that have a higher beta, and you have to understand beta's effect to understand what their effect will be on your portfolio.

You can have a negative beta too. (Some strategies do.) If beta is -1, your portfolio will move one-for-one in the opposite direction of the market. This can be good or bad depending on what you are looking for. A strategy with a beta of -1 would have a negative return if the market returned a positive return. If the market returned 10%, a strategy with a beta of -1 would return -10%. Short-selling has this type of correlation to the market.

Beta is just the market return, and really, anyone can get the market return by buying an index. Think about it. If you own a mutual fund and your returns just mirror the index, or worse, after fees, are less than the index, then what are you paying for? What you should be paying for is alpha.

Alpha measures the return of a strategy after adjusting it for beta or market risk. Alpha is really a measure of the true "value-added" by the manager. For example, if the return on your portfolio was 18% but your beta was 1 (i.e. the market also went up 18%), then no value was added to your portfolio by the manager. All of the return came from the movement of the market.

However, if your return was 18%, but beta (market return) was only 9%, your alpha is 9% (alpha = portfolio return less market return). Your manager, through his talents in managing the portfolio, added 9% to your bottom line. Now, that's impressive. That means that if you weren't invested with that manager and you were just invested in the index, your return would be half of what it is now.

You can actually have a negative alpha on a portfolio. If you ever come across a money manager that has a negative alpha, run the other way. A negative alpha means that the manager has actually "destroyed" value and has done worse than the market, without reducing your risk at all.

Traditional money managers (like mutual fund managers) are also aiming for alpha, but alpha is very difficult to achieve if you only have a hammer as your main tool. This goes back to our discussion of the differences between hedge fund managers and mutual fund managers.

Why is alpha important? Because the whole premise of hedge fund managers is to add alpha. Anyone can give you beta, it's really inexpensive. Just go out and buy an index fund and you will get the market return (i.e. the beta). Some of them have almost non-existent management fees. If you're going to pay a fee to a manager (hedge or mutual fund), make sure you are getting some kind of alpha.

Many people complain about fees. True, no one likes to pay fees, but I would venture to say that what people really have an issue with is fees in the absence of any value. I don't think people have an issue paying for something as long as they get value for it. If you get a return in your portfolio that is above and beyond the market return with less volatility, that's worth paying for.

4

Myths about hedge funds and Long-Term Capital Management

Hedge funds are often shrouded in mystery and confusion. Many people don't know what they are and only hear about them in the news when some sort of a negative event occurs. There is a lot to understand. As you can see, they are not as simple and straightforward as mutual funds. The fact that U.S. hedge fund managers don't have to report their holdings or register with the national securities regulators certainly contributes to the mystery. Mystery makes us suspicious because we tend to think, if someone isn't upfront about something, it must be bad.

There are several common myths surrounding hedge funds. Let's put them on the table and dispel them.

Myth: Hedge funds are risky and speculative

Some strategies may very well be considered risky if taken on their own, just as it would be considered risky if you weren't properly diversified in your portfolio and held only one technology company. But risky compared to what? Risky compared to watching your portfolio drop 40% in a "conservative blue-chip" equity fund? Of course, as with everything else, hedge funds involve risks, they're just different risks than what you may be used to in traditional investments. As you will see in Chapter 6, many hedge funds have lower volatility than traditional strategies and consequently, less risk.

There is a notion that sometimes the use of more sophisticated vehicles like short-selling and leverage might be speculative. Frankly, they are sometimes. But as we have seen with our examples of short-selling and leverage, these techniques can also be used to reduce the risk in a portfolio, just like our friend Jones did.

Don't hedge funds blow up?

You certainly may have that perception from reading some of the press coverage in the newspapers. Keep in mind as you read these stories that the job of newspapers is to sell stories. Unfortunately, they often focus on the negatives because that's what sells papers. Now, I want to point out that these stories are usually (though not always) accurate in their reporting of the news. However, from the way the information is presented, not to mention the frequency, you would think this happened on a weekly basis, and that's certainly not the case.

Because there is still an unfamiliarity and aura of mystery surrounding hedge funds (often for the reporters as well) it's much easier to create a negative image of the whole asset class, clump all hedge funds together and call them "bad".

That being said, I cannot deny that there aren't risks, or that there haven't been "blow-ups".

Long-Term Capital is a "blow-up" that still lingers in the minds of many investors

For those of you who aren't familiar with it, it was one of the most publicized, biggest, and most famous hedge fund disasters. Alan Greenspan and the Federal Reserve Bank actually intervened. It was in the news over and over again for several years.

It really is beyond the scope of this book to go into a long detailed analysis of what, why, where and whom, but it is important that you know the basics:

The fund was managed by a brilliant money manager, John Meriwether, with partners who were extremely prestigious on Wall Street, including PhD's and Nobel Laureates. These were not some kids just out of school; they all had brilliant reputations and track records in managing money.

Things got particularly difficult in 1998 with several financial disasters hitting all at once, including the Russian debt crisis and the Asian currency crisis. Long-Term Capital Management (LTCM) made some big bets and lost. The problems in a nutshell: leverage, risk and greed. Add those together and you have a disaster on your hands. Essentially, everything that could have gone wrong, did and that, combined with a disproportionate amount of leverage, is what did them in. The partners and current investors in the fund lost everything.

The strategy LTCM used primarily was "bond arbitrage", which is not terribly risky in and of itself. It would capitalize on small price differences of different bonds. If they bought a bond at 100, they would sell it when it got to 101, which doesn't seem like much of a profit at all, does it? But when you add leverage, it can be very significant. The problem was, financial crisis came unexpectedly in the markets and there was a huge flight to quality. Everybody jumped into T-bills for safety. Their trades went against them and to top it off, they were levered about 100 to 1.

The fund had operated in secrecy for fear of others trading against them or copying their trades. Long-Term Capital, like many hedge funds still today, lacked transparency; no one knew what they were holding in their portfolio. One problem was that the fund had done extremely well in the past, never losing money in any month. Long-Term Capital's founder Meriwether and the brains behind him were believed by Wall Street to walk on water, which is, of course, extremely dangerous. Wall Street banks and brokerages kept lending them money without any thought as to LTCM's ability to pay it back. The banks lent them money without collateral, which is very unusual. They did this because they all thought Long-Term Capital and the people behind it were golden.

The losses racked up and spiraled out of control until the Federal Reserve had to step in and force an intervention. Mr. Greenspan was livid and demanded that the banks and other financial institutions that had lent them the money so recklessly bail them out before more havoc rained on the already very nervous markets.

Had the Fed not stepped in, Long-Term Capital would have had to declare Chapter 11 bankruptcy and liquidate billions of dollars worth of positions it had on its books. This would have meant a complete wipeout of many investment dealers and the large banks and brokerages would have had significant losses on their balance sheets. An already very troubled market could have spiraled completely out of control.

By 1999, Meriwether and his partners had paid back close to 75% of the bank bailout. By 2000, most of the approximately $3.5 billion bailout had been repaid to the banks and brokerages who participated. Investors and partners of the fund lost everything they had invested.

How can you read about LTCM and not think that hedge funds are risky, speculative and could blow up? In general, they really aren't. Could this happen again? Maybe, but I doubt it. I think the institutions involved and the industry as a whole have learned to be more cautious and more rigorous with their "safety nets" and on-going due diligence.

Despite the myth that hedge funds are risky, they are known to be quite conservative vehicles in general. This is evidenced by the fact that pensions, foundations, and endowments are increasing their investments in hedge funds at a fast pace.

Would you put your money where billions of dollars of pension money is going?

Institutional investors invested approximately $175 billion in hedge funds in 2002 alone according to industry statistics. This compares with about $50 billion a few years earlier.

Look in any pension magazine and there is a substantial amount of space dedicated to hedge fund investing. Of course, pension funds have different investment objectives than you and I. Obviously, they have far more funds to work with, and they are also exempt from taxes. However, if you think about them, they are not just big, powerful mammoths of cash that make investment decisions. Pension funds represent thousands of *regular individuals' life savings*. Because of that, they tend to be conservative in their investment decisions.

There's a good chance that as you read this, you may already be participating to some extent in hedge funds through your pension plan, depending on where you work. The following are all pension plans and companies that invest in hedge fund strategies. Many of them are planning on increasing their allocation:

Yale Endowment Fund, California Public Employees' Retirement System (CalPERS, US's largest pension plan), Eastman Kodak, Nestle, IBM, Weyerhaeuser, Amoco, Zurich Insurance, Shell Canada, Ontario Municipal Employees Retirement Fund, Rogers Media, Pennsylvania State Employees' Retirement System, McGill University, General Motors. I could go on, but I think you get the picture.

Remember, all these institutions represent millions of individuals' life savings. Because they represent so many people and so much money they have to be very careful in their decision-making.

The pension plans of these institutions and many more have invested billions of dollars into hedge fund strategies. The individual allocations vary widely amongst institutions; some have just a small allocation, under 5%, while others, like the Yale Endowment Fund have over 25% of their portfolio allocated to hedge funds.

Why are these institutions invested so heavily in hedge fund strategies? Because they recognize the value of adding this asset class to their portfolios. They have done enormous amounts of research on the impact of adding hedge funds to their pension plans. They recognize the inherent qualities of diversifying away from the market and the lower volatility of returns that are characteristic of hedge funds. Many pensions that have added hedge funds have done so only since 2001-2000 being under pressure to make up large investment losses incurred by the market. That said, many pensions have been investing in strategies like these for many years without much publicity.

Here is an excerpt from a speech made by David Swensen, the Chief Investment Officer of the Yale University Endowment at the CMS New York Investment Seminar on November 25, 2002:

"We have close to 13 years of data on absolute return investing*. The driving principle behind our absolute return investments is that returns ought to be fundamentally uncorrelated with those of traditional marketable securities. In addition, over a reasonable period of time absolute return investments should provide returns that are commensurate with those that you might find in marketable securities. Over the period that we've managed this as a stand-alone asset class we have achieved both of those goals.

The returns of our absolute return portfolio have come in at 12.2% per annum and the correlation with domestic equities has been approximately zero for the thirteen years that we have been investing in the asset class. The standard deviation of returns has been about 6.5%, which is really quite striking given the standard deviation of returns for domestic equities over the last 75 years has been close to 20%."

* When Mr. Swensen refers to "absolute return investing", he is referring specifically to hedge funds.

Myth: Hedge funds are only for institutions or the super rich

At one point, this was true, but as the education level of investors and regulators increases, the barriers to entry are decreasing. More and more people are meeting the requirements of the accredited investor rules. In addition, many hedge funds, such as fund of funds, have significantly lower investment minimums than individual hedge fund strategies. Many hedge fund products are now becoming available under different product structures that allow for much lower investment minimums. (We'll go into some of these in a later chapter as well.)

So, hedge funds are not just for pensions and the super rich. They can be, in many ways, for anybody that invests. The one thing many institutions and ultra wealthy investors have in common is their desire and need for *"preservation of capital"* and a need for adding an asset class to their portfolio that diversifies away some of their traditional market risk they are already exposed to. That is what investing in hedge funds has brought them, and what it can bring you too.

Myth: Hedge funds are a fad

How can something be a fad if it's been around since 1949 and is being used as an investment vehicle by some of the largest, most prominent pension funds and companies in the world? Bell-bottom jeans are a fad. Alternative investment strategies that have been around for over 50 years are not. So, if someone tells you that hedge fund investing is a fad, I dare say they don't know what they're talking about. I hope you are realizing that hedge fund investing is truly not a fad, but an important investment diversification tool.

So, what are the lessons to be learned here? I think the main lesson here is to not avoid investing in hedge funds, because there is a lot of value to be gained from them. I hope you're beginning to see that. The real lesson is to educate yourself, know the potential risks, be cautious, and know what you're getting into. Is this a guarantee that nothing bad will happen? Of course not. But if you are cautious and educated, and diversify, you reduce your risk further and further.

Let's talk now about some of the risks involved in hedge fund investing.

5

Risks in hedge funds: What you need to know

I bet you wish we didn't have to have this section. Me too. We could just all invest in hedge funds and live happily ever after with our nice, consistent returns. But you know as well as I do that there are risks to every type of investment, including hedge funds.

How do you eliminate risk? I guess you could buy a T-bill and hide under your bed. Even then, you have the risk of inflation, taxes, and someone breaking into your house. You can't ever eliminate all investment risk. All you can do is manage the various risks to the best of your abilities. I'm going to give you the tools to do just that.

My 6 rules for managing investment risk:

1. Every investment has a risk associated with it: There is no return without some kind of risk, even if that risk is taxes, inflation, or the opportunity costs of doing something else. If you want the rewards of making an investment return, you have to take risk.

2. Only you know what level of risk you can handle: You are the one that has to sleep at night, so don't talk yourself, or let anyone else talk you into taking on more risk than you're comfortable with for the promise of outstanding returns. Unfortunately, sometimes we find out about our risk tolerance the hard way.

3. Ask a lot of questions: This is your money and you have the right to ask as many questions as you want. Keep asking questions until you're comfortable with the answers and you have a true picture of the risks involved. If someone tells you there are no risks, or very few risks, to investing in a particular strategy, they're likely lying. If they don't know the risks involved, that's a big red flag as well.

4. Find an investment strategy that has great risk discipline: If you can find a strategy with a consistent and rigorous approach to risk management, that will improve your odds of preserving and growing your capital.

5. Diversify: Spreading your risks out will produce more consistent returns. (You know this one already.)

6. Seek professional advice: Find someone who is knowledgeable to help you manage your risk, such as an advisor or a consultant. If investing isn't your full-time job, find someone who dedicates his or her life to it. Seek their help and their years of experience to help you properly evaluate the risks of investing in a particular vehicle.

Different kinds of risk

Dealing with risk certainly isn't an easy task, but it's one that you absolutely must do if you want to be a successful investor in hedge funds. Next, we are going to discuss some of the most common risks in hedge fund investing. Some of the following risks will be more prevalent in some strategies than in others, simply because of the nature of the strategy. When we discuss the various strategies in the next chapter, I will outline for you the most common risks that apply to each one. Some of these risks apply to traditional equities as well. All of these risks are manageable with the proper due diligence, which we'll discuss in Chapter 7.

You should keep something in mind as you digest all the potential risks there are: it's called a "risk premium". A risk premium means that you, as the investor, should be compensated for each risk that you take on. It's the same as wanting a better rate of interest if you're going to invest in Timbuktu Hydro Bonds rather than U.S. Government Bonds. You are facing a possible risk of default on the bonds and you should be compensated for that. It is no different with the list below.

Market risk: The market goes down

We spoke about this one earlier, this is beta risk. Market or beta risk is the risk of being tied to market returns. Market risk is lower in some hedge fund strategies, but higher in others that are largely correlated to the market. When we go through the strategies, you will see they are laid out according to their market risk, so you will have a clear picture of what the market risk is for each one.

Credit risk: The company goes bankrupt and can't honor its bonds

Credit risk is the risk of a company defaulting on their obligations because of a poor financial position. This risk applies usually only to bonds of companies, not their shares. For example, if you buy bonds from a company with a weak balance sheet, they'll likely pay you a great rate of interest to attract you as an investor. There's also a chance that they might run into financial hardship and not be able to pay back the money you lent them. This is called "defaulting". When you buy a company's bond, you are lending that company money and assuming they have the ability to pay it back to you. This type of risk would apply to hedge fund managers that buy corporate or high-yielding bonds.

Liquidity risk: You can't get your money back

We've touched on this one before. The more efficient a market, the higher the liquidity, but that also means fewer opportunities for the manager. Consequently, many of the securities managers invest in are not liquid, meaning they can't be sold at a moment's notice. If something happens and you need your money in a hurry it might be very difficult for the manager to sell off his trades and get your money back. If he does try to sell them off quickly he might not get a good price for them, which will affect your return. Since many of the securities hedge fund managers invest in are not liquid, that makes many strategies illiquid as well.

Asset-liability mismatch risk: The liquidity of the fund is different from the liquidity of the investments

We talked about how certain transactions, or holdings, in a hedge fund can be illiquid and may require several weeks or months to sell. What if the redemption policy, when you are allowed to sell your units of the fund, is weekly? You have to ask yourself this: If the fund is saying I can have my money in a week's notice, but the manager is holding investments that may require a month to sell, where are they getting my money from? Sometimes a fund will hold a cash reserve to meet redemption requirements, but that can dilute returns. A fund would offer you weekly liquidity as a way to try to get investors into the fund; they know people don't like to wait to get their investment funds back.

Event risk: An unpredicted event happens

Event risk is the risk of some kind of a negative, unforeseen event happening. Event risk is associated with global, unanticipated events that occur that are outside the control of the manager. An event like this might cause problems for the fund manager and adversely affect some of his existing or future positions because it was (1) unanticipated and, (2) has widely reaching negative effects. Examples of event risk would be: the Asian crisis, the Russian currency crisis, political upheaval, and 9/11.

Corporate event risk: Unexpected company news comes out

This is a risk specific to the companies the hedge fund manager might be investing in. For example, a manager has shorted a specific company because his research showed him that the company's stock should fall. Suddenly the company comes out with a positive earnings surprise that the manager was not expecting. Because of the positive earnings surprise, the shares go up in value and the manager loses money on his short sale. Corporate event risk applies to events of a company outside the manager's control that adversely affect his trades.

Manager risk: The manager thinks he can walk on water

This one is interesting, and is far more prevalent with hedge funds than with mutual funds. The mandates of managers who manage mutual funds have much stricter guidelines than those of hedge fund managers. We know this is one of the fundamental differences between hedge funds and mutual funds. Hedge fund managers, depending on the strategy, often have a lot more leeway to make investment decisions based on their own "gut" instinct.

Therefore, the actual actions of the manager can have a greater impact on the performance of a hedge fund than with mutual funds. This can work wonderfully well some of the time, but if the manager starts making big bets because he thinks he is invincible, that can turn into a big problem. In the hedge fund community, this particular manager risk is called "hubris".

Another manager risk is laziness or complacency. A new hedge fund manager might be harder working than one who is already established. I heard about one investor who tracked the number of vacation days his hedge fund managers took, and when they started to go up substantially after a few years, he sold the fund.

When you invest in a hedge fund, you're buying the manager to a large extent. You're buying the person because they have such a large influence over the risk and returns of the fund. When you buy a mutual fund, you usually invest in the company, and the strength of their brand name.

Pricing risk: It's difficult to price some securities

Because of the sometimes illiquid nature of the securities or derivatives that hedge fund managers invest in, it is often hard to put a price or value on these instruments. Illiquid securities are difficult to price because they are not traded very often, so the price someone is asking to buy it at (the bid price) could be very different from the price someone is willing to sell it at (the ask price). Sometimes you might hear about a "bid/ask spread" on shares of companies. That is the difference between the selling price and the buying price. It's hard to value shares if there is such a wide discrepancy between those two prices. So, for example, a manager might estimate the price of Vladimir Vodka at $2.00 a share, but when he actually goes to sell it, finds out it's really worth $1.50 a share.

Operational/administrative risk: People or systems risk

There is risk associated with systems or technology failure, as well as "people risk" associated with human error. For example, a trader executing a trade that a fund manager has asked him to put through could make a mistake and sell shares at the wrong price. That is just one of the many potential administrative or operational errors that could adversely affect your return. This can occur in mutual funds as well, but doesn't happen as often as with hedge funds, where trades are far more complex and there is more room for error. In addition, hedge funds don't usually have the large infrastructures that mutual funds do, which means there is sometimes less staff available to catch mistakes if they do occur.

Capacity risk: The manager takes in more money than he should

We touched on capacity issues earlier when we discussed the differences between hedge funds and mutual funds. Hedge funds, depending on their strategy, will have limited capacity for a given strategy. They can't take in more money than there are opportunities. If they do this, their performance is dampened and they lose a significant amount of their performance fees. For example, there may only be a certain number of deals to invest in during a specific time-frame. Capacity risk is the risk that a manager takes in more funds from investors, even though he really cannot manage the additional funds effectively. Although managers do worry about their performance fees, some might believe they can still achieve the same returns with more assets. This is perhaps a subset of "manager risk".

Model risk: The model being used has a glitch

There are some strategies that run on mathematical models or strict formulas instead of relying solely on the decisions of the manager. In these cases, there could be a problem or a "glitch" somewhere in the formula, which could adversely affect results. Sometimes formulas have holes in them that aren't visible until an unforeseen event occurs. It's kind of like driving around in your car with brakes that need fixing; you won't necessarily know your brakes need fixing until you need them. In addition, the model could have been based on flawed assumptions.

Counter party risk: Someone else involved in the transaction acts unfavorably

First, let's start by defining a counter party. A counter party is someone who is transacting with the fund manager on the other side of his trade. This can be anyone that the fund manager has an agreement with to complete a transaction. It can be a "prime broker" who actually executes the trade for the manager, or a company in Eastern Europe that has agreed to sell the manager its corporate bonds. So, for instance, if you bought a pair of jeans over the internet, your counter party risk is that the seller of the jeans won't deliver them to you, even though you've paid for them. Counter party risk is the risk that the other party won't deliver on its promise.

Leverage risk: The risk of borrowing too much

We talked about how leverage can be used in a conservative way to enhance returns. Not every fund uses leverage but many do, and a substantial amount, as we saw with Long-Term Capital Management, can be a disaster.

The prime broker who actually executes the trade for the manager usually needs some kind of collateral before they execute any trades. If something goes wrong, they don't want to end up paying for it themselves.

The risk is if the prime broker needed more and more collateral because the portfolio went down in value. This is called a "margin call" and I hope that you haven't experienced one. Banks or brokerages will lend you a certain amount of funds (or margin) based on the amount you have on deposit with them. If that amount goes down below a certain threshold, (because of adverse market movement or otherwise) you will be asked to put in more money.

Leverage isn't dangerous on its own. It's only dangerous when there is a margin call because the value of the securities has gone down. When you're heavily leveraged, you have borrowed all that money — it's not yours. To receive a margin call is hard, but when you're highly leveraged, it can be very dangerous.

The hedge fund manager can be in a similar situation and this can force a manager to incur substantial losses if he doesn't have the funds available to add to his account. If you receive a margin call and don't add the amount required, your position is sold at the current market price. Imagine if the bank where you have your mortgage called you tomorrow and told you they wanted all their money back by the end of the day. To come up with the money you might have to sell your house at a fire-sale price, at the worst possible time.

Fraud risk: The risk of unethical behavior

There are a few bad apples out there, but not as many as you think. It's hard to know what the exact number is. According to the recently published SEC report entitled "Implications of the Growth of Hedge Funds", since 1999, the SEC has brought approximately 38 enforcement actions relating to hedge fund advisors and hedge funds. The hedge fund universe is estimated to have between 6000-

7000 hedge funds worldwide. If we approximate 6500 hedge funds, 38 funds represents a 0.0058% fraud rate, or 99.9942% rate of "non-fraud". Even though not all hedge funds are governed by regulatory bodies, they are still subject to the anti-fraud provisions of the various investment acts.

The SEC even states in its report that, "There is no evidence indicating that hedge funds or their advisors engage disproportionately in fraudulent activity." They go on to say, "The fraud charged in Commission enforcement actions against hedge fund advisors has been similar to the types of fraud charged against other types of investment advisors… Finally, based on the Commission's recent cases, both registered and unregistered investment advisors have engaged in hedge fund fraud". This is definitely a risk, but the press coverage of events really gives you the impression that there is a lot more fraud than actually exists.

Data risk: You're not getting the true performance numbers

Unlike mutual funds that must report their returns and holdings with the securities regulators, hedge funds don't need to report their returns and positions. Because of this, it's difficult to get a clear, verifiable picture on what the hedge fund data is. Because they aren't obligated, not all hedge fund managers report their numbers. The results of hedge fund managers' cumulative performance depends a lot on what source you're using to get the figures from. Different databases will have different returns for a particular strategy, depending on who responds.

Another element of data risk is called "survivorship bias". Survivorship bias occurs when managers that have shut down and given clients back their funds are usually not included in the data base. This makes the returns a little bit higher than if they were included.

Another type of data risk is called "back-fill bias". This refers to a manager who won't report until he has a few great years. He will then want all the performance numbers over the last few years to be "filled in" from the years he hasn't reported. Now that the data looks great, he wants the data to be included, which gives a positive upward bias to the data. Yet another bias occurs when very successful hedge fund managers are not interested in taking in more money won't report to the data providers.

Legal/regulatory risk: A legal implication could ruin a deal

A legal or regulatory risk is a risk a hedge fund manager faces when a transaction or trade in his portfolio is dependent on a positive legal outcome, or regulatory approval. An example of a legal/regulatory risk hedge fund managers have to face occurs when managers invest in less developed countries. Because of the political instability that often exists in offshore or less developed countries, it is sometimes very difficult to enforce legal claims, should they arise. Another legal/regulatory risk is in the case of a strategy that involves profiting from a particular merger. If the appropriate authorities do not approve the merger, the trade unravels, and the investment is lost.

Style drift risk: The manager changes investment styles

A manager could start drifting to another investment style than the one you bought into. This is an issue because, presumably, you've evaluated all the risks involved with the particular strategy you're looking at. If that strategy changes, you might be faced with a whole new set of risks to deal with that you hadn't anticipated. Style drift risk often happens when capacity is reached on a particular strategy. The manager accepts more money than there are specific investment opportunities, and is then forced to take on a different style to deploy the funds. The manager may not have the requisite skill set to do that properly.

Lack of transparency: You can't see the manager's positions

Transparency is the ability to fully see: (1) what the investment approach is of the hedge fund manager, (2) what the processes are for implementing his approach, (3) what positions the hedge fund manager is holding in her portfolio and (4) what the fees and expenses are of the fund.

Mutual funds have high transparency because they are so heavily regulated. You can usually find out all of these things by going to their website anytime and downloading all the information you need. It's not an issue. For hedge funds it is. Let's go into some more detail about this particular risk.

Hedge fund managers aren't as open about their strategies and positions as mutual fund managers. As I mentioned, if you want to find out what stocks Blue-Chip Growth Fund has in its portfolio, you can go to their website and if it isn't listed, you can download them or go to any mutual fund tracking site and download from there. Granted, the information isn't up to the minute, it may only be updated monthly or quarterly, but it is still available.

There are two elements to the lack of transparency issue with hedge fund managers (1) they do not have to provide it (from a regulatory standpoint) and (2) they do not want to provide it. A hedge fund manager doesn't necessarily want you to know what they're holding in their portfolio. Why? For a couple of different reasons:

1. The manager believes (and is most probably right) that if someone finds out about their investment strategy, competitors will start to replicate it, particularly if the strategy is successful. Hedge fund managers make their returns and living off of implementing strategies that are often specialized and not widely know about. If competitors start to find out about a specialized "niche" strategy, the manager might lose their edge because a competitor could be capitalizing on all the good deals.

2. If competitors know what positions a hedge fund manager has, they can trade against them. This is akin to playing poker: you don't want your opponents to know which cards you're holding because they can use that against you. Conversely, if you know which cards they're holding, you can use that against them. For example, if you know what position your competitor is holding, you might try to "squeeze" them out of that position. This is done to not only cause them some grief, but also to potentially make money on their loss.

It doesn't sound fair, but if you knew your competitor was short XYZ Company shares, you might buy up some shares to push the price higher. When the price of the shares go up, the short position loses money and the manager has to get out of that position at some point since he can't continue to lose money on an on-going basis. If you keep buying shares, you push the price up and his loss gets bigger and bigger. At some point he will have to cover his short by buying XYZ shares, which you happen to own. You can then sell them to him at a higher price and you've made a profit. Essentially, when someone knows your position as a hedge fund manager, it puts you at a significant disadvantage.

But this secrecy is not fair, you still think. You're giving the manager your money, certainly you have a right to know his positions. Maybe you have a point, but much of the demand for transparency has to do with the perception that no transparency = risk or full transparency = no risk. That's really not the case, however.

Let's think about this for a second: if you had full transparency of the manager's positions, *what would you do with the information?* Would you be able to evaluate from a listing of securities what risks the manager was taking on? Would you want the list in order to try and replicate some of the manager's trades? What would you get from it exactly? I think there's a general perception that if you see holdings in a portfolio and you recognize the companies, you feel somewhat comforted: "Ah, yes, I've heard of Blue-Chip Company. They're a big company. The manager is holding it, that's good. I feel good."

The truth is, although having a listing of securities may tell you a lot about what the mutual fund manager is doing, it doesn't tell you *anything* about what a hedge fund manager is doing. Some industry experts even argue that it might even be a detriment to you if you had the information. For example, if you got a listing from a hedge fund manger that listed shares of ABC Company, T-bills, and DEF Company shares, you wouldn't know that the manager might be short ABC Company and long T-bills. You might think the opposite, decide to copy the trade, and end up losing money.

Having a listing of positions isn't a reflection of the trade the manager is putting on. Many hedge fund companies as well as their clients have embraced what the *true need for transparency is, and it's about risk.* They have adopted measures to provide risk transparency without providing position transparency. There are independent, third party companies that now provide this service of risk transparency, without revealing the managers' positions.

It is still an on-going debate in the hedge fund community. Clients want transparency and hedge fund managers are hesitant about giving it. Now, risk transparency is a compromise that both sides seem to be willing to settle on. There are more tools available now to present and evaluate the risks of a particular strategy, and more specifically the risks of every position, without revealing what the positions are. Having risk transparency, however, or any other kind of transparency, doesn't eliminate the crucial task of performing due diligence on a manager.

Let's talk about the different hedge fund investment styles, and then we'll move on to due diligence from there.

6

Hedge fund styles: What they are, how they've done

In traditional equity investing, there are different "styles" of investing and you probably already have a mix of them in your portfolio right now. If you own anything other than a government bond or guaranteed investment in your portfolio, you probably have investments with different styles or strategies; for example, having different geographic allocations (Canada, US, Japan, etc.), or a technology fund and a value fund.

Hedge funds, as we saw earlier, generally don't react the same way as traditional investments do to market changes. They generally have a low correlation to the market because of their inherent characteristics. Likewise, different hedge fund styles provide the next level of diversification within hedge funds as a group.

In the broad hedge fund category, there are many different kinds of hedge funds. Aggressive funds, conservative funds, hedge funds that are more correlated to the market, and hedge funds that are less correlated to the market. There are a few different ways to categorize these strategies but the most common way is by market exposure. If you're adding hedge funds to your portfolio to diversify away from the market, you should know how "exposed" to the market your hedge fund is.

Here are the strategies and where they fit in terms of their market exposure:

Low ◄——— Market Exposure ———► High		
Relative Value	**Event Driven**	**Opportunistic**
Convertible Arbitrage	Merger Arbitrage	Long/Short Equity
Fixed-Income Arbitrage	Distressed Securities	Global Macro
Equity Market Neutral		Short Bias
		Emerging Markets
		Managed Futures

I should point out that this does not represent the "Universally Accepted Hedge Fund Style Grouping"; there is no such thing. Analysts and consultants in the hedge fund industry have identified more than two dozen different hedge fund classifications. Some are extremely narrow and specific and represent a tiny portion of the hedge fund universe, and we won't be looking at them here. The strategies or styles listed above represent the most common strategies with the largest amount of assets. Categorizing hedge funds is difficult and subjective, based on the data that is available. Here is a breakdown of the size of each strategy in the approximately $600 billion hedge fund universe:

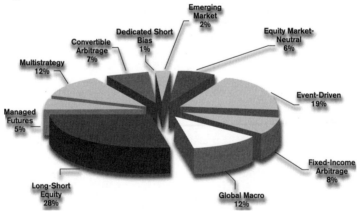

Source: CSFB/Tremont Index Weights as of September 2003

You will notice there is one on the pie chart called "multi-strategy" which we will not be discussed in detail here. It is simply a separate strategy that is a blend of other strategies.

Before I explain each of the styles and how they work, I have to tell you a little bit about where the data comes from.

Because the hedge fund universe is so different from the mutual fund universe, the ways of collecting data in the hedge fund world are quite different as well. Because hedge funds don't have the same reporting requirements as mutual funds, it is difficult to get an exact figure on the number of hedge funds in existence, and the total assets in the industry. Another issue in data collection is that hedge fund inclusion in the index is not mandatory, but *voluntary.* If a hedge fund doesn't want to report their performance figures to an index, they don't. Why wouldn't they? Well, if they had mediocre or negative performance figures they wouldn't want to be included. We spoke about this in the risks section under "data risk".

There are several hedge fund databases in existence today, but I use the CSFB/Tremont Index because I think they have the best methodology in compiling data for the index. The index is an asset-weighted index. Asset weighting means that the bigger a fund, the more of the index it represents. This is how the S&P 500 Index works. It wouldn't be representative at all for a junior mining company, to have as much weight in the index as a large blue chip company with millions of shares outstanding.

In addition, the CSFB/Tremont Index includes only audited funds with a minimum of $10 million in assets, and a minimum one-year track record. They try to minimize survivorship bias by not removing funds until they are liquidated or fail to meet the financial reporting requirements. You can read more about their methodology at www.hedgeindex.com.

I have divided the strategies by market correlation so that you see the differences in risk and return patterns between them.

You will notice strategies are divided into three basic categories: Relative Value, Event Driven and Opportunistic. These are the most common categories used in the industry. While the strategies are all different, the three categories try to sum up the types of investment techniques that the portfolio managers have in common in each category. We've already had a detailed discussion of the risks involved in investing in all hedge fund strategies. At the end of the discussion of each strategy, you will see the risks more common to that particular strategy. I am really simplifying here. Keep in mind that there are whole textbooks written on each of these strategies. Let's begin with the first one on the left: Relative Value.

Low ◄———	Market Exposure ———►	High
Relative Value	Event Driven	Opportunistic
Convertible Arbitrage	Merger Arbitrage	Long/Short Equity
Fixed-Income Arbitrage	Distressed Securities	Global Macro
Equity Market Neutral		Short Bias
		Emerging Markets
		Managed Futures

Relative Value Strategies

Relative value strategies are also often known as "market neutral". These strategies have very little or no exposure to the underlying equity or bond markets (zero beta) and are low on the volatility scale.

Relative value strategies make money by identifying mis-pricings of securities or financial instruments. That means that there are imbalances in the price that certain securities trade for on the market and what they're really worth. It also means there can be price discrepancies between one market and another.

For instance, the price of tea in China on the Chinese exchange can be slightly different from the price of tea on the New York exchange mainly because of the exchange rate between the U.S Dollar and the Chinese Yuan at any given time. For example, a pound of Chinese tea trades on the Chinese exchange for 8.0 Chinese Yuan and on the New York exchange for $1 U.S. But the actual exchange rate is one U.S. Dollar = 8.27 Yuan. In this case there is a discrepancy between the U.S. price for a pound of tea ($ 1), versus the price on the Chinese exchange ($0. 97). So what a relative value manager would do is simultaneously buy Chinese tea in China for $0.97 and sell it in New York for $1.00. In this transaction he would make $0.03 per share of tea.

That doesn't sound like a lot does it? Well, if you bought and sold 100,000 shares, your profit would be $3000, and if you add 30% leverage, it can be $3900. If you do this type of trading consistently, you can start to make a decent return.

Low volatility is the main defining quality of strategies in the relative value category, mainly because the mis-pricings or discrepancies are so small and are only there for a very short time. Relative value managers are conservative by nature. They aren't making huge directional bets with a substantial portion of the portfolio. They are making several, much smaller bets, and are using a prescribed amount of leverage to enhance their returns.

A manager implementing these types of strategies believes (rightly) that there is a long-term equilibrium or balance that exists between securities. In the short-term, however, there can be a pricing imbalance, if only for a few seconds, of which they can take advantage.

Financial markets are generally very efficient, meaning that they take news, digest it quickly, and it's reflected in the stock price almost right away. For example, if news comes out about a company missing their earnings target, the price of the company's stock will fall (if it's going to fall) pretty much right away. It won't have a delay of a week or even a day to be reflected in the price. It's almost instantaneous. That being said, there's always a tiny wrinkle that relative value managers can exploit. (Exploit means to take advantage of in order to make a profit.)

The price difference might only be a third of a cent, but if you have several of these transactions, and you add a small amount of leverage, you could have a decent return. Could you do this yourself? Couldn't anyone do this? You can if you surround yourself with dozens of computers, kept track of all the markets worldwide 24/7 and were able to pull the trigger quickly. You would need a whole lot of espresso, I would think. Let's talk about the three main Relative Value strategies: Convertible Arbitrage, Fixed-Income Arbitrage, and Market Neutral.

Convertible Arbitrage Strategy

This strategy focuses on convertible bonds of companies. A convertible bond is, as the name implies, a bond of a company that can be converted into a fixed number of shares of that company at a certain future date. Convertibles are a hybrid of stocks and bonds and as such have characteristics of both stocks and bonds: For example, the price of a convertible will decline less than the company's stock in a falling equity market, but will act like the stock in a rising equity market. Now why do these vehicles exist?

Let's say Jim the farmer wanted to raise more money to expand his chicken farm. He could do it mainly two ways: he could issue more shares of Jim's chicken farm, or he could issue corporate bonds. If he issues more shares, he would have to dilute his ownership in his own company by creating more shares (because when you own shares, you own a piece of the company). Jim doesn't really want to do that.

So, he could issue corporate bonds instead. In that case he would pay you, the bondholder, a rate of interest for essentially loaning him the money to grow his farm. Now, why would I buy Jim's bonds if I can buy bonds of Blue Chip Company? You wouldn't, unless there was a good reason to do so.

Jim, recognizing the competition around him, issues convertible bonds to entice you to invest in his farm business. You buy Jim's convertible bonds (and he pays you a reasonable rate of interest) knowing that in the future you can convert them into shares of Jim's farm if his business becomes very successful. Let's say the price that you are able to convert the bonds to shares is $2 per share. If one day there is a global shortage of chickens and Jim's company takes off, the price of the shares might go to $10 on the exchange where they are traded. At that point, you would convert your bonds to shares at the $2 price on the convertibles, then sell them on the exchange for $10, and make an $8 profit per share.

There are different convertible bond "covenants" depending on the convertible bond. Some companies issuing convertible bonds will allow you to redeem the shares when you want, while others may require you to redeem them at a specified price. The "bells and whistles" are slightly different, depending on the convertible bond. Convertible bonds are used as an extra incentive to get you to invest in the bonds of a particular company. It's kind of the icing on the regular bond cake.

That's how convertible bonds work. So, how does convertible bond arbitrage work? The convertible arbitrage manager would look for convertible bonds that exhibit some kind of mis-pricing, or are a very good deal for the convertible bondholder. For example, to attract investors some bonds might be priced at less than what they are really worth, or perhaps the conversion price for the shares is particularly low compared to what they will likely be worth in the future.

In convertible bond arbitrage, the fund manager would buy Jim's bond, and hedge himself by selling short Jim's company shares. They make interest on the bonds and potential profits on the decrease in price of the shares. Does that mean the manager believes the price of the shares will go down in the future? Not necessarily, he is hedging himself by shorting the stock. If he held the corporate bonds, and then bought the shares long, he wouldn't be hedging himself at all, he would be completely exposed to whatever was to happen to Jim's company, good or bad. He would also then be a long only manager.

In convertible bond arbitrage, no matter which way the market moves, the manager has a chance of profiting. If the equity market goes up, the manager will make money on the bond (remember that convertibles act like equities in a rising market) and lose money on the short sale. If the market goes down, the manager will lose money on the bond and make money on the short sale of the shares. How does the manager make a profit? Through those small mis-pricings or discrepancies. Let's take a look at how this strategy has done compared to the traditional indexes:

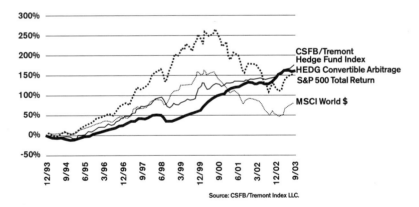

Source: CSFB/Tremont Index LLC.

$1000 invested in the convertible arbitrage strategy in 1994 would be worth $2616.20 by September 30, 2003. As you can see, it slightly underperformed the CSFB/Tremont Index but the returns were less volatile than the index as well.

Net Performance	HEDG Convertible Arbitrage	S&P 500 Total Return	MSCI World $
1 Month	1.97%	-1.06%	0.63%
3 Months	0.69%	2.65%	4.94%
6 Months	3.28%	18.45%	23.04%
1 Year	14.01%	24.40%	26.02%
2 Years	15.74%	-1.09%	2.25%
3 Years	31.20%	-27.42%	-26.25%
3yr Avg	**9.47%**	**-10.13%**	**-9.65%**
5 years	84.77%	5.08%	3.94%
5yr Avg	**13.06%**	**1.00%**	**0.78%**
Since Inception	161.62%	154.62%	81.59%
Incep Avg Annl	**10.37%**	**10.06%**	**6.31%**

Source: CSFB/Tremont Index LLC. Data as of September, 2003. Performance data is net of all fees. Index data begins January 1994. Sharpe ratio calculated using a rolling 90-day T-bill rate.

Year	HEDG Convertible Arbitrage	S&P 500 Total Return	MSCI World $
2003	**8.90%**	14.72%	16.96%
2002	**4.05%**	-22.10%	-19.54%
2001	**14.58%**	-11.89%	-16.52%
2000	**25.64%**	-9.10%	-12.92%
1999	**16.04%**	21.04%	25.34%
1998	**-4.41%**	28.58%	24.80%
1997	**14.48%**	33.36%	16.23%
1996	**17.87%**	22.96%	14.00%
1995	**16.57%**	37.58%	21.32%
1994	**-8.07%**	1.32%	5.58%

Source: CSFB/Tremont Index LLC. Data as of September, 2003. Performance data is net of all fees. Index data begins January 1994. Sharpe ratio calculated using a rolling 90-day T-bill rate.

Statistics	HEDG Convertible Arbitrage	S&P 500 Total Return	MSCI World $
Avg Month	0.84%	-1.06%	0.63%
Best Month	3.57%	2.65%	4.94%
Worst Month	-4.68%	-14.46%	-13.32%
Mth Std Dev	1.39%	4.59%	4.25%
Mth Std Dev, Ann'd	4.83%	15.92%	14.72%
Beta (vs S&P500)	0.04%	0.97%	0.85%
Sharpe	1.28%	0.37%	0.14%

Source: CSFB/Tremont Index LLC. Data as of September, 2003. Performance data is net of all fees. Index data begins January 1994. Sharpe ratio calculated using a rolling 90-day T-bill rate.

This strategy has a fairly high Sharpe ratio, which is good, and its beta is very small compared to the market.

Risks: The worse thing that can happen to this type of strategy is rising interest rates (market risk), which cause bond prices to fall, and a rising equity market. Luckily these two events don't usually happen at the same time. In addition, there is credit risk — the actual creditworthiness of Jim's company and his ability to pay back the bondholder. The manager has to balance looking for convertible bonds that pay a good rate of interest with their creditworthiness. Remember, it's the companies that have more risk associated with them that will pay a higher interest rate to entice investors to invest with them. Let's see how this strategy has done on the downside over time:

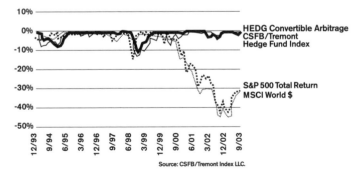

Source: CSFB/Tremont Index LLC.

Correlations	HEDG Convertible Arbitrage	S&P 500 Total Return	MSCI World $
Dow	0.09	0.93	0.89
MSCI World $	0.10	0.94	1.00
MSCI EAFE $	0.07	0.77	0.94
S&P 500 Total Return	0.12	1.00	0.94
NASDAQ	0.15	0.80	0.78

Source: CSFB/Tremont Index LLC. Data as of September, 2003. Performance data is net of all fees. Index data begins January 1994. Sharpe ratio calculated using a rolling 90-day T-bill rate.

The graph (on page 65) represents the "drawdowns" of the convertible arbitrage strategy since 1994 as well as the drawdowns of the traditional market indexes. A drawdown is simply the amount of loss (in percentage terms) in the portfolio from the highest point to the lowest point before a new high is reached. That sounds somewhat confusing, doesn't it? A drawdown percentage will tell you the amount of loss sustained when a portfolio drops until the time it bounces back again. This is a measure of the downside volatility of the portfolio and is also referred to sometimes as "peak-to-valley" drawdown.

This graph is useful because it tells you the magnitude of the worst drops in the strategy. It gives you a very good sense of what kind of volatility you can expect when investing in this strategy. The worst time for this strategy was in 1998. If you remember, 1998 was a particularly difficult time for both equity and bond markets because of the Russian currency crisis, among other negative market events.

Fixed-Income Arbitrage

This strategy uses the same principle of mis-pricings but with fixed-income vehicles. A fixed income vehicle is another term for different kinds of bonds. Often, mis-pricings will exist in the relationship between a Treasury (or government) bond and other kinds of bonds (i.e. corporate). Because U.S.T-bills are considered to be the world's safest securities, bond traders from all over the world use them as a standard or benchmark from which they can evaluate other more volatile bonds. The riskier the bond, the higher the rate of interest it offers. This of course makes sense because you need a higher rate of interest to compensate you for your risk.

The rate corporate bonds offer over government bonds of the same maturity is called the "spread". Spreads between different types of bonds are always changing based on a number of different factors: interest rates, the financial strength or creditworthiness of the company whose bonds are in the market, the price of the shares of the company, and many other factors. The fixed-income arbitrageur will find these disparities and trade on them before they come back into line.

This strategy will also exploit abnormalities in the "yield curve". A yield curve is a curve that matches up different government maturities of bonds with what yield they're paying. So logically, the 10-year government bond should be paying more interest than the 5-year government bond because you're putting your money away for longer, so they should compensate you more.

Sometimes there's a wrinkle in the yield curve. For example, a 7-year bond is actually yielding less than the 5-year bond. Why would this ever happen? Sometimes it's just a question of supply and demand. Imagine, for example, a whole bunch of fund managers decided they needed 7-year bonds for their portfolios. They run out and buy them, thereby pushing the yield on the 7-year bond down. (More demand pushes the price up, which pushes the yield down.)

At the same time, if no one wanted the 5-year bond, its yield would stay the same, or maybe even go up a little to attract buyers. In this situation, a fixed-income arbitrageur would buy the 5-year bond, because it was relatively cheap, and sell the 7-year bond because it was expensive, making a profit on the difference. (The price went up when the yield went down.)

There are several kinds of these arbitrage trades using different kinds of bonds: municipal, corporate, government, etc. Again, these aren't huge discrepancies and they're not there for very long, so you really have to move quickly as a fund manager. But if you have several of these trades in a portfolio and you add a small amount of leverage to enhance the return, you can achieve a decent return. Here's how they've done:

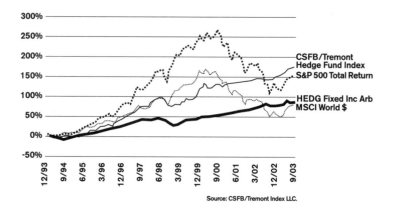

Source: CSFB/Tremont Index LLC.

This strategy has underperformed the CSFB/Hedge Index by quite a bit, but look at how smooth the line is. The volatility has been very low. $1000 invested in this strategy in 1994 would be worth $1897.30. This strategy hasn't done as well as the convertible arbitrage strategy we've explored so far, but the risk is even lower on this one. These are bonds after all, not equities. The efficiency of bond markets is usually quite high, so fewer as well as smaller mis-pricings occur than perhaps in other markets.

Net Performance	HEDG Fixed Inc Arb	S&P 500 Total Return	MSCI World $
1 Month	1.16%	-1.06%	0.63%
3 Months	0.38%	2.65%	4.94%
6 Months	3.28%	18.45%	23.04%
1 Year	4.47%	24.40%	26.02%
2 Years	13.86%	-1.09%	2.25%
3 Years	22.79%	-27.42%	-26.25%
3yr Avg	**7.08%**	**-10.13%**	**-9.65%**
5 years	38.80%	5.08%	3.94%
5yr Avg	**6.78%**	**1.00%**	**0.78%**
Since Inception	89.73%	154.62%	81.59%
Incep Avg Annl	**6.79%**	**10.06%**	**6.31%**

Source: CSFB/Tremont Index LLC. Data as of September, 2003. Performance data is net of all fees. Index data begins January 1994. Sharpe ratio calculated using a rolling 90-day T-bill rate.

Year	HEDG Fixed Inc Arb	S&P 500 Total Return	MSCI World $
2003	6.07%	14.72%	16.96%
2002	5.75%	-22.10%	-19.54%
2001	8.04%	-11.89%	-16.52%
2000	6.29%	-9.10%	-12.92%
1999	12.11%	21.04%	25.34%
1998	-8.16%	28.58%	24.80%
1997	9.34%	33.36%	16.23%
1996	15.93%	22.96%	14.00%
1995	12.50%	37.58%	21.32%
1994	0.31%	1.32%	5.58%

Source: CSFB/Tremont Index LLC. Data as of September, 2003. Performance data is net of all fees. Index data begins January 1994. Sharpe ratio calculated using a rolling 90-day T-bill rate.

Statistics	HEDG Fixed Inc Arb	S&P 500 Total Return	MSCI World $
Avg Month	0.56%	0.91%	0.60%
Best Month	2.02%	9.78%	9.06%
Worst Month	-6.96%	-14.46%	-13.32%
Mth Std Dev	1.16%	4.59%	4.25%
Mth Std Dev, Ann'd	4.00%	15.92%	14.72%
Beta (vs S&P500)	0.01%	0.97%	0.85%
Sharpe	0.65%	0.37%	0.14%

Source: CSFB/Tremont Index LLC. Data as of September, 2003. Performance data is net of all fees. Index data begins January 1994. Sharpe ratio calculated using a rolling 90-day T-bill rate.

Risks: There are two main risks; interest rate risk and credit quality risk. Bonds are adversely affected by an increase in interest rates. When interest rates go up, bond values go down. When interest rates move up quickly, it's usually because there is a financial crisis in the market and people rush out and buy T-bills, which are considered to be the safest investment around. This is called a "flight to quality". When this happens, the liquidity in many other investments (including other bonds) dries up and they are more difficult to sell. No one wants to buy anything other than a T-bill. This is why the strategy had such a large drawdown in 1998. Because of the Russian currency crisis and the Asian crisis, investors bought T-bills, and sold every other investment.

Because the fixed income arbitrage manager is looking at pricing discrepancies between different kinds of bonds, he may buy higher-yielding corporate bonds and be exposed to the credit risk associated with the company issuing the bonds.

Here is what the drawdown chart looks like:

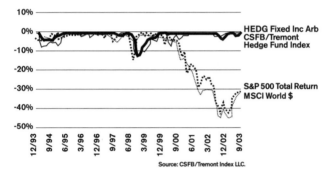

Source: CSFB/Tremont Index LLC.

Correlations	HEDG Fixed Inc Arb	S&P 500 Total Return	MSCI World $
Dow	0.04	0.93	0.89
MSCI World $	0.03	0.94	1.00
MSCI EAFE $	0.03	0.77	0.94
S&P 500 Total Return	0.03	1.00	0.94
NASDAQ	0.05	0.80	0.78

Source: CSFB/Tremont Index LLC. Data as of September, 2003. Performance data is net of all fees. Index data begins January 1994. Sharpe ratio calculated using a rolling 90-day T-bill rate.

Equity Market-Neutral

The name "market neutral" implies independence of the market, but aren't all hedge fund strategies supposed to be independent of the market? In theory, yes they are. In reality, there are certain strategies that are more correlated to the market. They're not 100% correlated obviously, but to some extent they are influenced by movements in the market.

Equity market neutral is designed to produce very consistent returns, low volatility and low (or no) correlation to the markets. The strategy, being a part of the relative value/arbitrage category exploits market inefficiencies as did the other two we looked at. While the first strategy we talked about uses convertible bonds, and the second uses fixed income, this one involves a "matched" portfolio of stocks. What this means is it has exposure to both long and short positions, just like a long/short strategy, but here, the positions are matched up one-for-one.

In a long/short portfolio, you can have 70% longs and only 30% shorts which makes a bigger bet on the direction of the market. In other words, you're more confident the market will rise. Not so with market neutral. If it is a perfectly matched portfolio of stocks, there is essentially zero (or very close to zero) exposure to the market. Market neutral would have 50% longs and 50% shorts, or zero beta. So, if the market goes up the portfolio makes money on the long positions and loses on the shorts, and vice-versa. If it all balances out, how do they actually make a profit?

It comes down to the specific companies they're holding, and to the manager's skill at buying the companies that are more likely to go up, and shorting the companies that are more likely to go down within the same sector. For example, even though the manager might have exposure to all the sectors of the market (financials, gold, technology, etc.), there will be some companies that he thinks will do better than others in that same sector. Based on that, he may go long ABC financial and short XYZ financial. This is appropriately called "pairs trading". The manager will not do this randomly; he will go long on the companies he feels will go up, and short the companies he feels will be more likely to go down in value.

Another type of market neutral strategy is called "statistical arbitrage", which is a more quantitative way of doing "pairs trading". "Stat arb", as it is often called, looks at the statistics, the numbers, and the technical charts versus the fundamentals of the company. The manager will still be market neutral in the financial sector overall, so even if there's a big hit to the sector, whatever he loses on the long side, he'll make up on the short side.

It's that little spread on the two companies that creates the return. Add several small spreads, a small amount of leverage, and you have a reasonable return with very little volatility. No market exposure and no net sector exposure. If the share prices do not move at all, you will still be making a small amount (the T-bill rate interest rate) on the funds you collected from selling shares short.

This is a conservative strategy so if you're looking for something to light your socks on fire, it's not going be a market neutral strategy. If, on the other hand, you like sleeping well at night, this may be more appropriate. Let's see how the strategy has done over all:

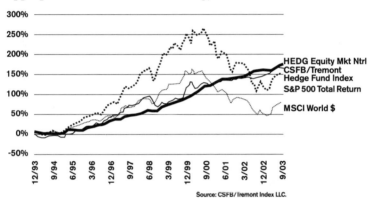

Source: CSFB/Tremont Index LLC.

Look at how smooth the returns line is. $1000 invested in market neutral in January 1994 would be worth $2699.70 at September 30, 2003. This strategy has by far the highest Sharpe ratio of all the strategies, 2.10.

Net Performance	HEDG Equity Mkt Ntrl	S&P 500 Total Return	MSCI World $
1 Month	1.06%	-1.06%	0.63%
3 Months	1.80%	2.65%	4.94%
6 Months	3.94%	18.45%	23.04%
1 Year	6.65%	24.40%	26.02%
2 Years	14.47%	-1.09%	2.25%
3 Years	26.27%	-27.42%	-26.25%
3yr Avg	**8.08%**	**-10.13%**	**-9.65%**
5 years	73.24%	5.08%	3.94%
5yr Avg	**11.62%**	**1.00%**	**0.78%**
Since Inception	169.97%	154.62%	81.59%
Incep Avg Annl	**10.72%**	**10.06%**	**6.31%**

Source: CSFB/Tremont Index LLC. Data as of September, 2003. Performance data is net of all fees. Index data begins January 1994.
Sharpe ratio calculated using a rolling 90-day T-bill rate.

Year	HEDG Equity Mkt Ntrl	S&P 500 Total Return	MSCI World $
2003	**5.03%**	14.72%	16.96%
2002	**7.42%**	-22.10%	-19.54%
2001	**9.31%**	-11.89%	-16.52%
2000	**14.99%**	-9.10%	-12.92%
1999	**15.33%**	21.04%	25.34%
1998	**13.31%**	28.58%	24.80%
1997	**14.83%**	33.36%	16.23%
1996	**16.60%**	22.96%	14.00%
1995	**11.04%**	37.58%	21.32%
1994	**-2.00%**	1.32%	5.58%

Source: CSFB/Tremont Index LLC. Data as of September, 2003. Performance data is net of all fees. Index data begins January 1994. Sharpe ratio calculated using a rolling 90-day T-bill rate.

Statistics	HEDG Equity Mkt Ntrl	S&P 500 Total Return	MSCI World $
Avg Month	0.86%	0.91%	0.60%
Best Month	3.26%	9.78%	9.06%
Worst Month	-1.15%	-14.46%	13.32%
Mth Std Dev	0.90%	4.59%	4.25%
Mth Std Dev, Ann'd	**3.10%**	**15.92%**	**14.72%**
Beta(vs S&P 500)	**0.07**	**0.97**	**0.85**
Sharpe	**2.10**	**0.37**	**0.14**

Source: CSFB/Tremont Index LLC. Data as of September, 2003. Performance data is net of all fees. Index data begins January 1994. Sharpe ratio calculated using a rolling 90-day T-bill rate.

Risks: Manager risk: The manager might get his stock selection wrong and be long ABC and short XYZ when it should have been the other way around. Short-selling borrow risk: the stock actually has to be available for you to borrow to be able to sell it short and sometimes, it's not. Liquidity risk: it's not easy to sell a particular stock sometimes. If there aren't a lot of shares in circulation, it's more difficult and you don't always get the best price.

How did this strategy do on the downside? As you can see, not too badly at all. Because market neutral is so well balanced (50% longs, 50% shorts) its hard to lose a lot of money in this strategy. The returns and losses are fundamentally based on the manager's stock picking ability.

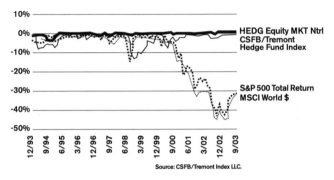

Source: CSFB/Tremont Index LLC.

Correlations	HEDG Equity Mkt Ntrl	S&P 500 Total Return	MSCI World $
Dow	0.40	0.93	0.89
MSCI World $	0.37	0.94	1.00
MSCI EAFE $	0.31	0.77	0.94
S&P 500 Total Return	0.40	1.00	0.94
NASDAQ	0.29	0.80	0.78

Source: CSFB/Tremont Index LLC. Data as of September, 2003. Performance data is net of all fees. Index data begins January 1994. Sharpe ratio calculated using a rolling 90-day T-bill rate.

We've now covered the relative value category. Let's sum up briefly what we've learned so far:

- Relative value strategies are the least correlated to traditional equity markets.
- They work by finding small discrepancies in the markets and profiting from them, before they come back into market equilibrium.
- They are the least volatile strategies of all hedge fund strategies.
- Although they are not the overall best performing strategies of the group, they tend to have the highest Sharpe ratios because of their low volatility component.

Let's move on to our second category of hedge funds: the Event Driven strategies.

Low	← Market Exposure →	High
Relative Value	**Event Driven**	Opportunistic
Convertible Arbitrage	**Merger Arbitrage**	Long/Short Equity
Fixed-Income Arbitrage	**Distressed Securities**	Global Macro
Equity Market Neutral		Short Bias
		Emerging Markets
		Managed Futures

Event Driven Strategies

As you can see, we're moving further along the line towards higher market exposure. Event driven strategies are more correlated to the market than their relative value counterparts. As such, they have higher volatilities associated with them but the returns tend to be higher as well.

These types of strategies focus on finding securities of companies that can benefit (or falter) from a certain future event. The focus is on companies that are being taken over, restructured, or going bankrupt. In addition, it may include companies that may be created through a spin-off or that are undergoing some other metamorphosis. Where there's change, there's usually an opportunity. The event driven fund manager will try to take advantage of valuation disparities or mis-pricings produced by these corporate events.

The fortunate thing is, these events are less dependent on the market. Imagine a big merger deal that has been in the news. The deal has been announced but is still a few months away. The market dropping 100 points won't change the deal going through. However, in times of real financial crisis, the relationship between these strategies and the market tends to gets closer, as you will see through some of the returns and drawdown charts of the strategies.

Let's look at two of the major event driven strategies in this category: merger arbitrage and distressed securities.

Merger Arbitrage

This is also known as Risk Arbitrage, or "'Risk Arb". Merger arbitrage managers focus on locking in a profit when a merger deal is announced. Usually, when a company proposes to take over or merge with another, they will pay a higher price for the shares of the company they want to buy than what those shares are currently trading at. Presumably, the merger will create synergies and economies of scale, which will eventually influence their own bottom line and share price.

When a merger of a company is announced to the public, the shares of the company being acquired or taken over usually go up. On the flip side, the acquiring company's shares will usually go down. Buying another company will cost money, putting pressure on their balance sheet, which pushes the stock lower. A merger arbitrage manager usually thinks the deal will go through and places trades based on the movement in share price of the two companies involved. Let's look at an example.

Elephants Company wants to grow so it decides to take over Mice Company by proposing to buy up all their shares. Elephants Co. knows that once the two companies are combined, they will be far more profitable than they are today. So, it offers to pay a higher price of the shares of Mice Co. than what they are selling for on the market. Mice Co. thinks it's a good deal, and agrees to the offer.

After the merger is announced to the public, the shares of Mice Co. go up in value to reflect the premium or increased bid that was placed on them. Arbitrage fund managers are also buying up shares of Mice Co. thinking the deal with go through and eventually the price of the Mice Co. shares will move towards the price the Elephants Co. offered to pay for them.

The deal itself may take months to complete, but as soon as it is announced to the public, the shares of Mice Co. will go up. They won't go up as much as the Elephants Co. offer because there's always a chance the deal won't go through. If the deal doesn't go through, the shares will come back down in value and everyone knows that. Consequently, arbitrageurs are cautious about what they pay for shares.

There are many reasons why a proposed deal would not go through such as, regulations, shareholder approval, or another competing offer. The target company may come out with a negative earnings surprise during the course of the deal and its stock could drop, making the acquiring company withdraw its original offer. Another reason may be that the market itself thinks it's a bad deal and pushes the stock price of Mice Co. down far enough (by selling the shares) to the point where the Elephants withdraw their original bid. On the flip side of that, it could be such a good deal that another competitor, often known as a "white knight", comes in with a better offer for the Mice Co. which they may decide to take. These are just a few examples of "deal-killers".

How does a merger arbitrage manager profit from this potential deal? They do the following: they will sell short the shares of the company doing the acquiring (Elephants Co.) and buy the shares of the company being bought (Mice Co.). In effect, they are buying up the shares that will go up in value and selling short the shares of the company that will go down in value. We talked earlier about the acquiring company's balance sheet being affected, so think of it as a huge purchase on their company Visa that will negatively affect their share price.

Usually companies won't pay for other companies with the cash in their bank accounts. They will usually pay for at least part of the acquisition with shares of their company. When this happens, they will issue new shares, so the existing shares get diluted. Having more shares outstanding, means each share is now worth less, so the price of the shares drop. At the same time, other arbitrage managers are in the market shorting the shares for a similar trade, pushing the stock down even further.

The arbitrage manager believes that the deal will close. If the deal doesn't close, he'll lose money on the trade. In that case, the shares he has short (Elephants) will go up in value as others buy the shares to cover their shorts. The shares he has long (Mice) will probably go down in value because the company is not as valuable now that it is not being acquired.

Some managers who are confident a deal won't go through will do the reverse trade - buy the Elephants, sell the Mice. As the merger date draws closer, the spreads of the prices of the two companies converge. They get closer and closer because the chance of the deal not going through gets smaller and smaller. Remember that the movement in the share price of these two companies is tied with a bungee cord from the time they make the announcement of the merger until the time the deal actually closes.

Once the trades have been placed, a good risk arbitrage manager will carefully monitor the progress of the deal. They can't just close their eyes and wait until the end. If it looks like the deal might not go through for one of the reasons we talked about, or for another reason, they have to decide quickly how to salvage their trade to avoid as much loss as possible.

If the spread between the prices of the two companies widens that means the market thinks the deal isn't going through and it is reflected in the share prices of both the companies. Widening spreads are bad news for merger arbitrage managers. It means they will likely lose on the deal, because it doesn't look as if the deal is going to go through. Let's look at an example:

Elephants Co. stock trades at $50, Mice Co. trades at $18. The Elephants offer the Mice 0.5 an Elephant share for each Mice share. (That's a good deal because 0.5 an Elephant share is worth $25.) The value of the deal is then $25 a share for the Mice.

When the deal is announced, the following happens: Elephant shares drop to $48 (due to fear of dilution) and Mice shares go up to $21 from its original $18 (due to the premium Elephants are offering and the anticipated economies of scale from the upcoming merger).

So, what a merger arbitrage manager would do is sell short 50 Elephant shares betting that they will fall farther. At the same time they would buy 100 shares of Mice at $21, anticipating it will rise to $25. What they have done is locked in a profit based on the price movement of the shares of each of the companies and the ratio of the share exchange between them. (Elephants are offering 1/2 of each of their shares worth $25, but the Mice are only trading at $21 after the Mice shares go up in the market from $18.)

Let's see how merger arbitrage strategies have done overall:

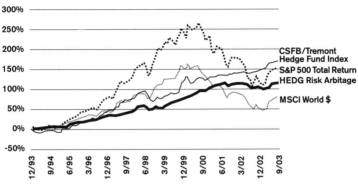

Source: CSFB/Tremont Index LLC.

Net Performance	HEDG Risk Arbitrage	S&P 500 Total Return	MSCI World $
1 Month	0.95%	-1.06%	0.63%
3 Months	2.61%	2.65%	4.94%
6 Months	7.63%	18.45%	23.04%
1 Year	7.50%	24.40%	26.02%
2 Years	4.01%	-1.09%	2.25%
3 Years	10.52%	-27.42%	-26.25%
3yr Avg	**3.39%**	**-10.13%**	**-9.65%**
5 years	49.27%	5.08%	3.94%
5yr Avg	**8.34%**	**1.00%**	**0.78%**
Since Inception	118.67%	154.62%	81.59%
Incep Avg Annl	**8.36%**	**10.06%**	**6.31%**

Source: CSFB/Tremont Index LLC. Data as of September, 2003. Performance data is net of all fees. Index data begins January 1994. Sharpe ratio calculated using a rolling 90-day T-bill rate.

Year	HEDG Risk Arbitrage	S&P 500 Total Return	MSCI World World $
2003	**6.16%**	14.72%	16.96%
2002	**-3.46%**	-22.10%	-19.54%
2001	**5.68%**	-11.89%	-16.52%
2000	**14.69%**	-9.10%	-12.92%
1999	**13.23%**	21.04%	25.34%
1998	**5.58%**	28.58%	24.80%
1997	**9.84%**	33.36%	16.23%
1996	**13.81%**	22.96%	14.00%
1995	**11.90%**	37.58%	21.32%
1994	**5.25%**	1.32%	5.58%

Source: CSFB/Tremont Index LLC. Data as of September, 2003. Performance data is net of all fees. Index data begins January 1994. Sharpe ratio calculated using a rolling 90-day T-bill rate.

Statistics	HEDG Risk Arbitrage	S&P 500 Total Return	MSCI World $
Avg Month	0.68%	0.91%	0.60%
Best Month	3.81%	9.78%	9.06%
Worst Month	-6.15	-14.46%	-13.32%
Mth Std Dev	1.30%	4.59%	4.25%
Mth Std Dev, Ann'd	**4.51%**	**15.92%**	**14.72%**
Beta(vs S&P 500)	**0.13**	**0.97**	**0.85**
Sharpe	**0.92**	**0.37**	**0.14**

Source: CSFB/Tremont Index LLC. Data as of September, 2003. Performance data is net of all fees. Index data begins January 1994. Sharpe ratio calculated using a rolling 90-day T-bill rate.

Risks: We've talked about some of the risks of this strategy already. The main risk is the deal not going through because the manager (or arbitrageur) is placing trades, betting that it will go through. When a merger fails, the long position that is being held (in this case, Mice Co.) drops significantly because it is not considered as valuable any more.

It's very important that an arbitrage manager has a diversified portfolio of these deals to offset some "failed" deals. To offset the risk of a failed deal, a manager will place his trades on the two companies after the deal is already announced. Some managers will place trades on a potential or rumored deal, but this is considered speculation.

There is some short-risk here too because it might be hard to borrow the stock they want to short. Here is how this strategy has done on the downside:

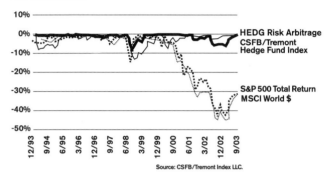

Source: CSFB/Tremont Index LLC.

Correlations	HEDG Risk Arbitrage	S&P 500 Total Return	MSCI World $
Dow	0.44	0.93	0.89
MSCI World $	0.45	0.94	1.00
MSCI EAFE $	0.43	0.77	0.94
S&P 500 Total Return	0.43	1.00	0.94
NASDAQ	0.39	0.80	0.78

Source: CSFB/Tremont Index LLC. Data as of September, 2003. Performance data is net of all fees. Index data begins January 1994. Sharpe ratio calculated using a rolling 90-day T-bill rate.

As I think you're beginning to see from the downside graphs, 1998 was a bad year for just about every hedge fund strategy.

Distressed Securities

This second event-driven strategy focuses on investing in companies that (just as the name suggests) are or are expected to be, in trouble or distress. Distressed managers will invest in distressed securities. Why would anyone want to do that? For the potential of finding a diamond in the rough.

Distressed managers rely on extensive research and evidence to show which companies are currently undervalued but really have long-term potential and can be turned around. If the company does turn around, then a handsome profit can be made.

This is not a strategy where a fast profit can be made. This involves long-term (or sometimes really, really long-term) investments in very illiquid bonds or shares of companies. The shares are illiquid in this case because there will be no other buyers for a company that is perceived to be in distress.

When a company is on the brink of bankruptcy or is in bankruptcy full-force, investors obviously head for the hills and dump their shares on the market for whatever they can get. Large public and private pensions will dump their shares too, not necessarily because they want to, but often because of their strict investment guidelines (i.e. most can't own "junk" status bonds). What can happen in this case is that the price of the security may fall below what it's really worth.

It may seem odd that a company in bankruptcy can continue to function or operate as it did and eventually come out of bankruptcy to potentially make a profit for its investors. Many investment managers will actually be active in the company's turnaround, hoping of course to recoup their investment.

Distressed securities fund managers perform exceptional due diligence on the companies before they invest; most of the deals they invest in do very well. The only downside for the managers is the length of time it takes to get a return or payback on their investment. This strategy has less correlation to events of the market. Once a company is bankrupt and in distress, the market going up, down or sideways won't change its bankrupt state. It also won't change all the re-structuring work involved in getting back on its feet again. Let's see how they've done:

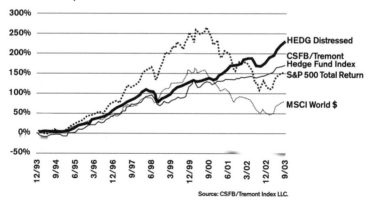

Source: CSFB/Tremont Index LLC.

As you can see, they've done quite well. $1000 invested in 1994 in distressed securities would be worth $3347.40. On the flip side there are more drawdowns in this strategy overall compared to the other strategies. The worst monthly drawdown on record is -12.45%. That's a substantial monthly drop. Could you handle it?

Net Performance	HEDG Distressed	S&P 500 Total Return	MSCI World $
1 Month	2.21%	-1.06%	0.63%
3 Months	4.43%	2.65%	4.94%
6 Months	13.19%	18.45%	23.04%
1 Year	24.37%	24.40%	26.02%
2 Years	24.02%	-1.09%	2.25%
3 Years	40.59%	-27.42%	-26.25%
3yr Avg	12.03%	-10.13%	-9.65%
5 years	86.97%	5.08%	3.94%
5yr Avg	13.33%	1.00%	0.78%
Since Inception	234.74%	154.62%	81.59%
Incep Avg Annl	13.19%	10.06%	6.31%

Source: CSFB/Tremont Index LLC. Data as of September, 2003. Performance data is net of all fees. Index data begins January 1994. Sharpe ratio calculated using a rolling 90-day T-bill rate.

Year	HEDG Distressed	S&P 500 Total Return	MSCI World $
2003	19.17%	14.72%	16.96%
2002	-0.69%	-22.10%	-19.54%
2001	20.01%	-11.89%	-16.52%
2000	1.95%	-9.10%	-12.92%
1999	22.18%	21.04%	25.34%
1998	-1.68%	28.58%	24.80%
1997	20.73%	33.36%	16.23%
1996	25.55%	22.96%	14.00%
1995	26.12%	37.58%	21.32%
1994	0.67%	1.32%	5.58%

Source: CSFB/Tremont Index LLC. Data as of September, 2003. Performance data is net of all fees. Index data begins January 1994. Sharpe ratio calculated using a rolling 90-day T-bill rate.

Statistics	HEDG Distressed	S&P 500 Total Return	MSCI World $
Avg Month	1.06%	0.91%	0.60%
Best Month	4.10%	9.78%	9.06%
Worst Month	-12.45	-14.46%	-13.32%
Mth Std Dev	2.04%	4.59%	4.25%
Mth Std Dev, Ann'd	**7.07%**	**15.92%**	**14.72%**
Beta(vs S&P 500)	**0.23**	**0.97**	**0.85**
Sharpe	**1.27**	**0.37**	**0.14**

Source: CSFB/Tremont Index LLC. Data as of September, 2003. Performance data is net of all fees. Index data begins January 1994.
Sharpe ratio calculated using a rolling 90-day T-bill rate.

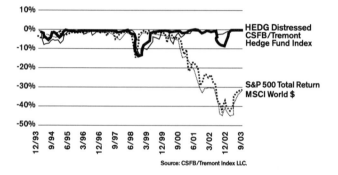

Source: CSFB/Tremont Index LLC.

Correlations	HEDG Distressed	S&P 500 Total Return	MSCI World $
Dow	0.53	0.93	0.89
MSCI World $	0.57	0.94	1.00
MSCI EAFE $	0.52	0.77	0.94
S&P 500 Total Return	0.54	1.00	0.94
NASDAQ	0.49	0.80	0.78

Source: CSFB/Tremont Index LLC. Data as of September, 2003. Performance data is net of all fees. Index data begins January 1994.
Sharpe ratio calculated using a rolling 90-day T-bill rate.

Risks: The risks of this strategy are mainly company specific; for example, the credit risk of the company, the risk of the company defaulting on its debt, or the risk of the company not coming out of bankruptcy. This is a strategy that shines only when a company is able to overcome its state of distress. Low liquidity is another risk.

Reorganizations and turnarounds of companies in distress typically can take a year or more. Constant, on-going monitoring is crucial to this strategy; this would be considered manager risk.

Event Driven strategies have the following characteristics:

- They perform better in general then relative value strategies.
- Their volatility and drawdowns are higher than relative value strategies.
- Their correlations to traditional equity markets are higher than relative value.
- Their Sharpe ratios tend to be lower than relative value.

Now, let's move on to our final category of strategies, Opportunistic Strategies.

Low	← Market Exposure →	High
Relative Value	Event Driven	**Opportunistic**
Convertible Arbitrage	Merger Arbitrage	**Long/Short Equity**
Fixed-Income Arbitrage	Distressed Securities	**Global Macro**
Equity Market Neutral		**Short Bias**
		Emerging Markets
		Managed Futures

Opportunistic Strategies

This is the group of hedge fund strategies that have the highest correlation to the market. Because they are highly correlated to the market, these strategies have the highest (or lowest) betas and consequently are the most volatile. Because of the high beta and high volatility these strategies tend to have a lower Sharpe ratios. Higher volatility means, of course, that they also have the highest probability of outstanding returns. If you're looking for high-octane strategies, shop in this category.

Long/Short

This is the most common strategy in the hedge fund industry today. About 28% of all hedge funds use this strategy according to CSFB/Tremont Index data as of September 30,2003. The popularity of this strategy is partially a function of its ease in understanding it: you have longs and then you have shorts. There are no complex mergers or arbitrage going on here. Some have done well, others have not done as well. It takes a special skill and talent to put on short sales and do it effectively. It's not the same skill as buying companies long.

This is a directional strategy. The manager is making a bet on a company and by doing that, is backing it up with a position in his portfolio. Essentially, he is buying (holding long) companies that are undervalued or are doing exceptionally well in their field and selling the shares of companies that are overvalued or are underperforming. Buying winners and selling losers.

A long/short fund that is perfectly balanced in terms of its longs and shorts (or perfectly hedged, with no market exposure) is essentially a market-neutral fund. Long/short funds are not perfectly hedged, however. There is usually a long bias in the majority of long/short funds. You can think of long/short as the aggressive cousin of market neutral.

There are many different long/short strategies. There are plain vanilla long/short funds that have no specific sector focus. Then there are sector specialist long/short managers that focus on regions (long/short Europe or long/short Japan) or sectors (long/short technology, long/short financials).

Unlike traditional long only managers, long/short managers can switch around from value to growth stocks, from small, medium or large companies. They can go from a net long position (i.e. they have more long than short positions) to a net short position (more shorts than longs). You might, however, run into a long/short fund that has a very strict discipline in the way it invests. Different long/short funds may have very specific mandates as to what kinds of companies they can and can't invest in. However, most long/short funds are quite flexible to invest however they see fit.

As most of their investment mandates are flexible, so are the range of returns from this strategy. You can own one of these funds and be up 107% in a year, and your poor next-door neighbor can be down 57% with another long/short fund.

As we've talked about, this strategy is highly correlated to the market. In a rising market, the long/short strategies with a long focus will do better. In a declining market, the short-focus funds do better because the gains on the shorts will be bigger than the losses on the longs. Let's see how they've done:

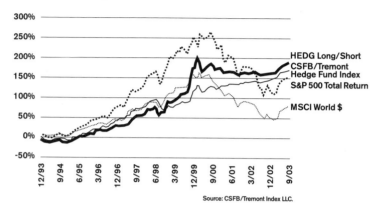

Source: CSFB/Tremont Index LLC.

Notice how the return line is starting to look more like the S&P 500 and the MCSI Index? That is because it is more correlated to the market.

Net Performance	HEDG Long/Short	S&P 500 Total Return	MSCI World $
1 Month	1.21%	-1.06%	0.63%
3 Months	2.54%	2.65%	4.94%
6 Months	9.76%	18.45%	23.04%
1 Year	11.48%	24.40%	26.02%
2 Years	9.83%	-1.09%	2.25%
3 Years	1.05%	-27.42%	-26.25%
3yr Avg	0.35%	-10.13%	-9.65%
5 years	76.15%	5.08%	3.94%
5yr Avg	11.99%	1.00%	0.78%
Since Inception	195.18%	154.62%	81.59%
Incep Avg Annl	11.74%	10.06%	6.31%

Source: CSFB/Tremont Index LLC. Data as of September, 2003. Performance data is net of all fees. Index data begins January 1994. Sharpe ratio calculated using a rolling 90-day T-bill rate.

Year	HEDG Long/Short	S&P 500 Total Return	MSCI World $
2003	9.92%	14.72%	16.96%
2002	-1.60%	-22.10%	-19.54%
2001	-3.65%	-11.89%	-16.52%
2000	-2.08%	-9.10%	-12.92%
1999	47.23%	21.04%	25.34%
1998	17.18%	28.58%	24.80%
1997	21.46%	33.36%	16.23%
1996	17.12%	22.96%	14.00%
1995	23.03%	37.58%	21.32%
1994	-8.10%	1.32%	5.58%

Source: CSFB/Tremont Index LLC. Data as of September, 2003. Performance data is net of all fees. Index data begins January 1994. Sharpe ratio calculated using a rolling 90-day T-bill rate.

Statistics	HEDG Long/Short	S&P 500 Total Return	MSCI World $
Avg Month	0.98%	0.91%	0.60%
Best Month	13.01%	9.78%	9.06%
Worst Month	-11.43	-14.46%	-13.32%
Mth Std Dev	3.21%	4.59%	4.25%
Mth Std Dev, Ann'd	11.12%	15.92%	14.72%
Beta(vs S&P 500)	0.42	0.97	0.85
Sharpe	0.68	0.37	0.14

Source: CSFB/Tremont Index LLC. Data as of September, 2003. Performance data is net of all fees. Index data begins January 1994. Sharpe ratio calculated using a rolling 90-day T-bill rate.

Some of the risks involved with this strategy are of course market risk (because it is highly correlated to the market), as well as company specific risk, and risks connected to short-selling and leverage. Let's see how they've done on the downside:

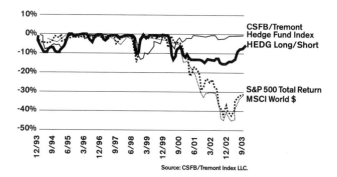

Source: CSFB/Tremont Index LLC.

Correlations	HEDG Long/Short	S&P 500 Total Return	MSCI World $
Dow	0.45	0.93	0.89
MSCI World $	0.61	0.94	1.00
MSCI EAFE $	0.56	0.77	0.94
S&P 500 Total Return	0.58	1.00	0.94
NASDAQ	0.76	0.80	0.78

Source: CSFB/Tremont Index LLC. Data as of September, 2003. Performance data is net of all fees. Index data begins January 1994. Sharpe ratio calculated using a rolling 90-day T-bill rate.

Again, you can see how it's more correlated to the traditional market indexes on the downside as well, and it has more of a drawdown than the CSFB/Tremont Index as a whole. You will notice, however, that even though the drawdowns occur more often than the other strategies, they are still far better compared to the traditional indexes.

Global Macro

Global macro managers will hold long and short positions in any of the world's major capital or derivative (futures/options) markets. They will have views on the market's overall direction and make trades accordingly. They will take advantage of changes in global events or trends. Global events and trends could be for example; changes in interest rates in Malaysia, the decrease of the Canadian dollar against the Russian ruble, the rise in the price of pork bellies. etc. "Macro" means "top down", so a macro manager will look down at the global economy with a bird's eye view and see where the opportunities lie. This is in contrast to a "bottom up" approach where a manager will look at company specifics first, and then look at where they fit in the overall global landscape.

The portfolios of these funds can include stocks, bonds, currencies and commodities, or derivative instruments; they can hold anything. Most funds invest globally in both developed and emerging markets. Global macro managers aren't at all restricted in their mandates. They can use any of the strategies we've talked about to make a profit: convertible arbitrage, merger arbitrage, long/short, etc., or techniques that are more specialized. They can do whatever they think will be profitable without much investment restriction.

Because global macro managers can do just about anything to make a profit, the strategy is very volatile. Lots of leverage, lots of glory, high stakes, big bets, big potential losses.

Ever heard of a man named George Soros? George is a big star in the hedge fund industry. He was a global macro manager who made a fortune (and history) shorting the British pound against the U.S. dollar in 1992. And when I say fortune, I mean $1 billion U.S. How did he do it?

In 1992, Soros shorted the British pound against the U.S. dollar. He did this because he believed the currency was over-priced compared to the U.S. dollar, and he thought that the Bank of England wouldn't be able to support the pound's price for much longer. Sometimes when a central bank wants to support a currency so that it is traded for a higher price on the global exchange, they will buy up that currency. Because there are fewer "dollars" in circulation, the price goes up.

Soros borrowed British pounds and sold them short. Soros was right, and the Bank of England couldn't support the pound anymore. When they stopped supporting it, the currency fell into a free fall and lost 20% of its value almost overnight. Soros now had a short position with a currency that was now 20% cheaper then when he sold it. Soros bought the pounds back at the cheaper price, and gave back the pounds he had borrowed. Because he used a substantial amount of leverage, the profit he made was substantial: $1 billion U.S.

The losses on this strategy can be just as spectacular as well. It is estimated that Soros sold short $10 billion pounds. Had the currency gone up instead of down, his losses could have been even more spectacular than his profit.

If you're comfortable with big roller coaster rides, this is what you'll get with global macro. The returns have been excellent for global macro funds as a group.

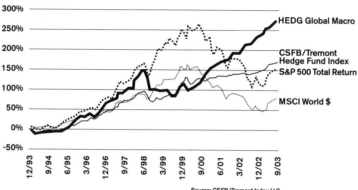

Source: CSFB/Tremont Index LLC.

Net Performance	HEDG Global Macro	S&P 500 Total Return	MSCI World $
1 Month	3.04%	-1.06%	0.63%
3 Months	4.27%	2.65%	4.94%
6 Months	11.47%	18.45%	23.04%
1 Year	18.35%	24.40%	26.02%
2 Years	36.33%	-1.09%	2.25%
3 Years	72.22%	-27.42%	-26.25%
3yr Avg	**19.87%**	**-10.13%**	**-9.65%**
5 years	65.30%	5.08%	3.94%
5yr Avg	**10.57%**	**1.00%**	**0.78%**
Since Inception	277.36%	154.62%	81.59%
Incep Avg Annl	**14.59%**	**10.06%**	**6.31%**

Source: CSFB/Tremont Index LLC. Data as of September, 2003. Performance data is net of all fees. Index data begins January 1994. Sharpe ratio calculated using a rolling 90-day T-bill rate.

Year	HEDG Global Macro	S&P 500 Total Return	MSCI World World $
2003	10.50%	14.72%	16.96%
2002	3.04%	-22.10%	-19.54%
2001	4.42%	-11.89%	-16.52%
2000	4.85%	-9.10%	-12.92%
1999	23.43%	21.04%	25.34%
1998	-0.36%	28.58%	24.80%
1997	25.94%	33.36%	16.23%
1996	22.22%	22.96%	14.00%
1995	21.69%	37.58%	21.32%
1994	-4.36%	1.32%	5.58%

Source: CSFB/Tremont Index LLC. Data as of September, 2003. Performance data is net of all fees. Index data begins January 1994. Sharpe ratio calculated using a rolling 90-day T-bill rate.

Statistics	HEDG Global Macro	S&P 500 Total Return	MSCI World $
Avg Month	1.20%	0.91%	0.60%
Best Month	10.60%	9.78%	9.06%
Worst Month	-11.55	-14.46%	-13.32%
Mth Std Dev	3.54%	4.59%	4.25%
Mth Std Dev, Ann'd	12.26%	15.92%	14.72%
Beta(vs S&P 500)	0.19	0.97	0.85
Sharpe	0.85	0.37	0.14

Source: CSFB/Tremont Index LLC. Data as of September, 2003. Performance data is net of all fees. Index data begins January 1994. Sharpe ratio calculated using a rolling 90-day T-bill rate.

$1000 invested in this strategy in January 1994, would be worth $3773.60 today. This is the best performing strategy we've looked at so far. As you can see, however, they finished some years off with a negative return.

Risks: After looking at those returns you probably don't want to hear a thing about the risks. The risks in this strategy, just like the returns, are large. Because global macro managers invest in many different instruments (companies, currencies, derivatives, etc.) the risks are dependent on what type of instrument is used. It is safe to say this strategy has all the risks of all hedge fund strategies put together:

market risk, liquidity risk, event risk, corporate risk, foreign exchange risk, credit risk, fraud risk, regulation risk, etc.

The biggest risk in this strategy, however, is manager risk. The manager dictates many of the other risks involved by the size of the bets he makes. Remember, if a macro manager feels strongly enough that interest rates in Indonesia are going to fall, he can use the whole portfolio to short Indonesian interest rate futures. Macro managers can, and do, place large trades based on their beliefs of certain economic or macro events. The risks and the rewards are high.

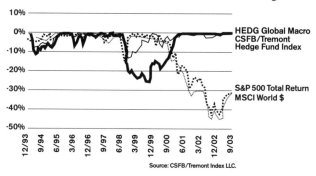

Source: CSFB/Tremont Index LLC.

Correlations	HEDG Global Macro	S&P 500 Total Return	MSCI World $
Dow	0.21	0.93	0.89
MSCI World $	0.19	0.94	1.00
MSCI EAFE $	0.12	0.77	0.94
S&P 500 Total Return	0.23	1.00	0.94
NASDAQ	0.19	0.80	0.78

Source: CSFB/Tremont Index LLC. Data as of September, 2003. Performance data is net of all fees. Index data begins January 1994. Sharpe ratio calculated using a rolling 90-day T-bill rate.

As you can see, this strategy has many drawdowns, and far worse than for any of the strategies we've seen so far. This strategy's worst drawdown came in 1998-9, not surprisingly.

Short Bias (Dedicated Short Selling)

This strategy represents a tiny percentage of overall strategies (about 1%) so we're only going to talk about it briefly. By now, we know what short selling is. Having a dedicated short-bias means your portfolio is more heavily weighted in short positions.

Because of the huge market run of the '90's (remember way back in the good old days) short sellers haven't done all that well as a group. Their performance is very much the opposite of the direction of the equity market as short selling is negatively correlated to the market. Not surprisingly, returns in 2000-2002 were excellent.

Short selling was the only strategy that produced positive returns in autumn of 1998, but it's one of the few hedge fund strategies that is more volatile than long only. Let's see how they've done overall:

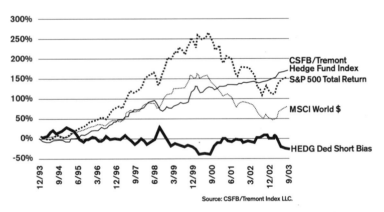

Source: CSFB/Tremont Index LLC.

No, this isn't the drawdown chart, it's the returns chart. Clearly not very impressive. If you look closely, you can see it's almost the opposite image of the traditional equity indexes. Remember, it is very difficult for this strategy to make money when stocks are going up, which they did for most of the nineties. On the flip side, however, this is one of the only strategies that has a negative correlation to equity markets.

Risks: The risks in this strategy are not dissimilar to the risks of investing in long-only strategies: market risk and stock specific risk. If you thought the upside chart was not that attractive, look at the downside chart:

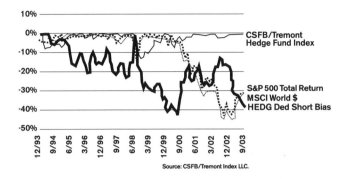

Source: CSFB/Tremont Index LLC.

Emerging Markets

This strategy also represents a very small amount of overall strategies (about 2%) so we won't go into as much detail as the other strategies. Generally, emerging markets strategies in the mutual fund world or the hedge world are volatile. If you've ever invested in emerging market mutual funds, you know the bumpy ride they offer.

Emerging markets are far less developed markets in general as well as financially. They place a very high importance on building up their economy and their capital market system. Because of this, they allow very limited short selling and don't offer real futures contracts to control risk. What this means is that emerging market strategies have a strong long bias.

Emerging markets hedge funds are restricted by not really being able to offer the full range of tools the other strategies have available to them such as short selling, futures, etc. This makes the strategy even more volatile.

Risks: The risks are the same ones involved with traditional long only investments in emerging market strategies: difficulty getting information, poor accounting, lack of proper legal systems, political and economic turmoil. Also, poor liquidity means lots of opportunity, but lots of risk. Look at the roller-coaster rides:

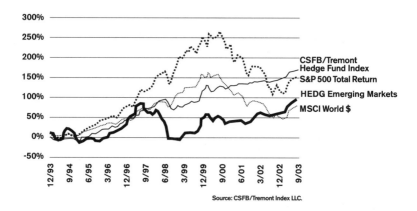

Source: CSFB/Tremont Index LLC.

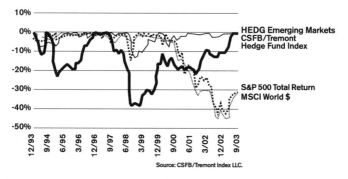

Source: CSFB/Tremont Index LLC.

Managed Futures

Some industry practioners don't consider managed futures as a hedge fund strategy, but a distinct strategy, not part of the hedge fund universe. It is often considered a stand-alone alternative investment strategy, such as real estate. That's why, if you pick up another book on hedge funds, you might not find a chapter on managed futures. While many of the characteristics of managed futures and hedge funds are different, many are the same.

I think it's important to include a description in this book, because the use of managed futures does allow for greater diversification in your portfolio, and I consider it to be a hedging strategy, even if not always viewed as a hedge fund.

Compared to the other hedge fund strategies we've seen, managed futures are more liquid, more transparent and regulated. They have their own governing bodies that monitor and audit them. Most managed futures funds are still subject to the accreditation rules, however, because they do not register their funds with the appropriate regulators.

Managed futures have almost an inverse correlation to the markets, and generate returns by going long and short on various futures contracts.

So what's a future? A future is a forward contract that trades on an exchange. When you buy a forward, just as the name implies, you're buying (or selling) it's price forward or in the future, for example in 3 months time. You're buying or selling today, but you're delaying the actual delivery of that "thing" to the future.

It's like the delay between the time you find a deal on a vacation, negotiate all the terms (where you are going, where you will stay, the price and payment) and the time you actually go on the vacation, which may be several months in the future. However, to take the analogy one step further, once you've planned and paid for your vacation, there is no turning back. If for some reason you can't go on the vacation, you won't get your money back. You still have to pay for it.

With futures, if you promise to sell someone 3000 pork bellies in 6 months, you are obligated to come up with those pork bellies in 6 months when the buyer shows up at your door looking for them.

You can buy or sell futures on many things, not just commodities like pork bellies; for example, you can have futures on currencies, interest rates, or equity indexes. Buying a futures contract on an asset gives you the same effect on your portfolio as owning the asset outright. So, buying a future on gold, is the same as buying gold, in terms of the financial effect on your portfolio. If gold goes up by 10% so does your futures contract, if it goes down 10% so does your contact, it's a one-for-one ratio.

This is quite different from an option: *When you buy an option, you have the right to buy something in the future at a pre-determined price, but you don't have to.*

If, for instance, you thought ABC Company was going to sky-rocket, you would buy options on ABC for $50 in 3 months, even though it's trading at $45 today. Why? Well if you thought the shares were going to go to $55, you could exercise your options at $45 (buy the shares at $45) and sell them in the market for $55, making a nice profit.

Why wouldn't you just buy the shares? You could, but you can buy options with a lot less money down. You can buy an option on shares for approximately $1 *whereas each share would cost you $45 today. Buying an option gives you financial leverage because you are putting down far less money and you can still participate in the movement of the share price.*

If the market went down, your option would expire worthless because you wouldn't want to exercise it at a higher price than what it was in the market. You would only lose the cost of the option, a $1 or so.

Futures markets can be used for investing or for hedging a price risk; the hedger is trying to reduce her risk, while the investor is trying to increase her return on her investment. Futures markets provide a mechanism for its participants to control price risk in their particular commodity or currency.

The hedgers in the futures market are in the market to **protect themselves** against adverse swings in the price of their particular goods. The investors (the fund managers) are there to take that risk away from the hedgers and be compensated for it. Futures prices are not a prediction of the future; they are an indication of what risks the producers and consumers of that good need to protect themselves against.

So, for example, if a jewelry manufacturer faces the risk of rising gold prices that would make it more expensive for him to buy the gold he needs to make his jewelry, he would hedge himself by buying gold futures. He benefits from gold prices going down so he would hedge himself by doing the opposite and go long on gold futures (just like you would hold a stock long).

With whom would he lock in his price? Who would take the other side of the trade? Well, that could be a gold miner. The gold miner fears gold prices will go down, so he hedges himself by going short gold futures. It's a little confusing but whatever your risk is, you would hedge yourself to that risk. So if your risk is the price of gold falling, you go short gold futures in case it falls. If your risk is the price of gold going up, you go long futures. Both the gold miner and the jewelry manufacturer are considered to be "hedgers".

If the gold miner wanted to sell more gold than the jewelry manufacturer wanted to buy, there would be a shortage in gold demand that someone needs to be willing to buy. An investor would do it. An investor's role is to balance out the needs of the producers and consumers. In this case it would be gold. An investor is sometimes referred to as a "speculator", because he is not a hedger. They will often take the other side of the trade, provide needed liquidity and *mitigate the price risk of the producers and consumers of the goods.*

Here's how it would work: if the price of gold goes up, the jewelry manufacturer profits on his long futures positions, which make up for his losses in having to buy the gold at a higher price to make the jewelry. If the price of gold goes down, the gold miner makes money on his short positions, making up for his losses at selling the gold from his mine at a lower price.

For every long position in the futures market, there's a short position. In fact, the positions of the hedgers and the investors are mirror images of each other; for every winner there's a loser, which is quite different from investing in stock and bond markets. If you buy shares of a company and they go up, it doesn't mean that someone else lost money on those shares. Not so in the futures markets. So, if that's the case, how do futures managers make a profit?

Investors (the futures managers) are compensated through trading profits for taking the price risk away from the producers and the consumers of the goods. That implies that the gold miner and jewelry manufacturer are often the losers on the trade if investors are making money. That is often the case, and that is the price they pay in exchange for having someone else take on their price risk. Remember, the hedgers (the miner and the manufacturer) are in the market to protect themselves against adverse swings in the price of their particular goods. That protection has a price, and that is the profit on the other side of the trade. The more hedged they are against price risk in what is essentially their main business (producing or mining gold, for example), the less they care about the losses on their futures contracts, which are offset by the gains on their goods.

Managed futures managers are often called CTAs which stands for "commodity trading advisors". Most futures managers fall into this category which means they use a "trend-following methodology", an automated computer system that follows trends in the futures markets and tells the managers when to buy or sell. A futures manager doesn't make a bet on whether something is over or undervalued, they just take on the risk the hedger isn't willing to bear, and get paid for it.

Futures have very little correlation to the regular equity markets, and are often negatively correlated to falling equity markets, so they've done very well since 2000 as you can see:

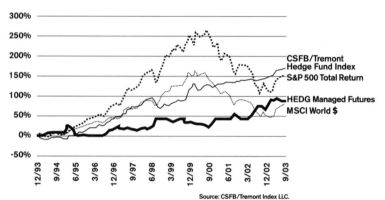

Source: CSFB/Tremont Index LLC.

Net Performance	HEDG Managed Futures	S&P 500 Total Return	MSCI World $
1 Month	-1.60%	-1.06%	0.63%
3 Months	-3.30%	2.65%	4.94%
6 Months	0.81%	18.45%	23.04%
1 Year	4.83%	24.40%	26.02%
2 Years	22.04%	-1.09%	2.25%
3 Years	49.25%	-27.42%	-26.25%
3yr Avg	**14.28%**	**-10.13%**	**-9.65%**
5 years	30.79%	5.08%	3.94%
5yr Avg	**5.52%**	**1.00%**	**0.78%**
Since Inception	85.46%	154.62%	81.59%
Incep Avg Annl	**6.54%**	**10.06%**	**6.31%**

Source: CSFB/Tremont Index LLC. Data as of September, 2003. Performance data is net of all fees. Index data begins January 1994. Sharpe ratio calculated using a rolling 90-day T-bill rate.

Year	HEDG Managed Futures	S&P 500 Total Return	MSCI World $
2003	**6.86%**	14.72%	16.96%
2002	**18.33%**	-22.10%	-19.54%
2001	**1.90%**	-11.89%	-16.52%
2000	**4.24%**	-9.10%	-12.92%
1999	**-4.69%**	21.04%	25.34%
1998	**20.64%**	28.58%	24.80%
1997	**3.12%**	33.36%	16.23%
1996	**11.97%**	22.96%	14.00%
1995	**-7.10%**	37.58%	21.32%
1994	**11.95%**	1.32%	5.58%

Source: CSFB/Tremont Index LLC. Data as of September, 2003. Performance data is net of all fees. Index data begins January 1994. Sharpe ratio calculated using a rolling 90-day T-bill rate.

Statistics	HEDG Managed Futures	S&P 500 Total Return	MSCI World $
Avg Month	0.59%	0.91%	0.60%
Best Month	9.95%	9.78%	9.06%
Worst Month	-9.35%	-14.46%	-13.32%
Mth Std Dev	3.52%	4.59%	4.25%
Mth Std Dev, Ann'd	**12.19%**	**15.92%**	**14.72%**
Beta(vs S&P 500)	**-0.18**	**0.97**	**0.85**
Sharpe	**0.19**	**0.37**	**0.14**

Source: CSFB/Tremont Index LLC. Data as of September, 2003. Performance data is net of all fees. Index data begins January 1994. Sharpe ratio calculated using a rolling 90-day T-bill rate.

Their performance over the long-term isn't as impressive as over the short-term, but as you can see from the correlation chart on page 102, they have a negative correlation to the markets.

Risks: Managed futures are very leveraged by nature. You can buy a $100,000 futures trade with only $10,000 (10% down). If the trade goes well, that's great. But if it goes down 20% because of the one-for-one ratio effect in your portfolio, you would lose your original $10,000 and have to come up with another $10,000. Manager risk is not a big risk here because most of the futures trading strategies are based on models, so a bigger risk would be model risk.

As you can see from the drawdown chart below, some of these risks often translate into negative returns. This is a volatile strategy, but it's a good diversifier for your portfolio because it has a negative correlation to equities.

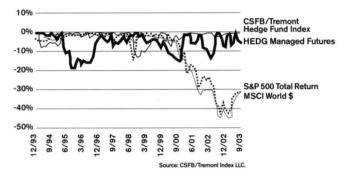

Source: CSFB/Tremont Index LLC.

Correlations	HEDG Managed Futures	S&P 500 Total Return	MSCI World $
Dow	-0.25	0.93	0.89
MSCI World $	-0.20	0.94	1.00
MSCI EAFE $	-0.13	0.77	0.94
S&P 500 Total Return	-0.25	1.00	0.94
NASDAQ	-0.25	0.80	0.78

Source: CSFB/Tremont Index LLC. Data as of September, 2003. Performance data is net of all fees. Index data begins January 1994. Sharpe ratio calculated using a rolling 90-day T-bill rate.

Now, that we've gone over the investment styles, let's move on to due diligence and see what you need to ask before you invest in any strategies.

7

Due diligence: Questions you need to ask

Because of the loosely regulated environment, almost anybody can set up a hedge fund. Combine that with potentially very lucrative performance fees, and you have an industry that attracts the best and worst talent at the same time. *You must separate the wheat from the chaff if you ever hope to be successful investing in hedge funds.* That's what due diligence is all about.

An industry survey was done among institutional investors and found that more than 50% of institutions took at least 2-6 months to complete their due diligence before they invested any money in a hedge fund. Okay, so you're not an institution, but the amount of time they take should give you an indication as to the amount of time and effort involved in due diligence. This isn't an area you can skimp on, the risks are just too great.

Due diligence is about all the research you have to do before you place one dollar with a hedge fund manager. Because of the less regulated environment that hedge funds live and breathe in, the onus of asking these due diligence questions comes down to you, my friend. You have to know absolutely everything about that hedge fund manager and their operation before you invest. It's not the same as investing in a mutual fund, or with another traditional investment manager where they've been vetted by regulators. When you buy a mutual fund you are often buying a brand name fund. You're relying on their reputation to find a good portfolio manager for your fund. When you buy a hedge fund you are buying the manager.

As we saw, there are risks specific to hedge funds that *you absolutely must be clear on before you invest.* You have to know the manager and the operation of that hedge fund inside out and backwards. Remember, when you buy a hedge fund, you're buying a hedge fund manager's skill. You're buying their specific expertise in exploiting different market inefficiencies. You're buying their years of experience at managing this specific strategy. You're buying their background, integrity, and ability to manage growth in their operation.

You are also buying that person's possible inability to manage the fund properly if he is ill, or is grieving for a lost loved one. You need to know everything, and to prepare yourself for anything. I'm telling you this now, because you might look at some of the questions that follow and think, "That seems a little ridiculous. Why on earth would I need to know that?"

You have to know whose track record you are buying when you buy a hedge fund — sometimes it's not the manager's. If a manager had a great track record but their staff turned over every 6 months, wouldn't that concern you? What if the person who executes the trades for the manager is actually responsible for most of the performance because the fund manager is out fishing every day? What if the manager fires him? Who is responsible for those numbers? You have to know that before you invest. This is just one example of what you must find out with due diligence.

The more you know about the hedge fund manager before you invest, the more you will understand and be able to properly evaluate if you want to take one of those particular risks. Proper due diligence is not a guarantee that a negative event won't ever happen, but it will significantly lower the risk of it happening. Or, I'm sure the option is still open to buy that T-bill and hide under your bed...

We are going to go through a list of detailed due diligence questions next. The following are questions you should ask and have answered by the hedge fund manager.

Unfortunately, these are not questions you have to have answered only once. This is a process you must do on an on-going basis. Due diligence is a full-time job. That is why I advocate that if you don't have one already, find someone who can help you do the work, like a qualified financial planner, advisor or consultant. Or hire a fund of funds manager, which we'll talk about in the next chapter.

Let's take a look at what questions need to be asked in order to reduce as much risk as you can from your investment decision. There are two parts to an effective due diligence process:

- Quantitative due diligence, which is looking at the numbers and the strategy.
- Qualitative due diligence, which is finding out about the manager and the hedge fund company.

Quantitative due diligence: Looking at the numbers

Looking at the numbers means more than just looking at the past returns. In addition to past returns, here are some things you should look at specifically:

1. Volatility of the fund: What is the fund's monthly, weekly, or daily volatility? Do the returns jump around all over the place, or are they consistent? Of course, it depends on the strategy you're going to invest in, *but if you think you're investing in a fairly conservative fund, there shouldn't be a lot of volatility of returns.*

2. Annual return: Was an annual return generated by large gains in one or two months? Or was the annual gain spread evenly across the period?

3. Negative performance: How bad were the worst months? By examining a fund's worst months you can determine if the fund matches your own risk tolerance. If the fund once lost 10% in a month and you think that's a lot, then the fund may not be for you.

4. Resilience: If the fund lost money, how long did it stay down, and how long did it take to recover? Why did a recovery occur? Did the manager change his or her strategy? Or did market conditions improve?

5. Even profit or home run: Did the manager make an even profit in all the positions in the portfolio? Or did he or she hit a home run on one trade that accounted for the majority of the gains of the fund in a particular period? Again, this depends on why you're going into the fund. If you're not looking for home runs, but small consistent movements, then this is important. What if the trade was a fluke and your manager has no real talent even if the returns are great?

6. Repetition: Is the fund's investment process easily repeatable? Or, did an isolated incident cause the fund to report good performance? For example; consolidation in the banking industry in the U.S. lead to great returns for hedge funds that were primarily long bank stocks. The consolidations turned out to be a one-time event, and when they were over the returns of those hedge funds suffered.

7. Strategy: Can you describe the fund's strategy? Ask yourself how the fund differentiates itself from others in its category. How are investment decisions made? What was the weakest investment? How was it sold, or was it? Can you describe the buy/sell discipline? Is there a buy/sell discipline? If you can't describe it, you probably don't understand it, which is okay as long as you have someone helping you to do this.

8. Strategy specific risk: Ask the manager what risks there are in his or her strategy. When the answer is "none" or "it's hard to tell", this can be a big red flag.

9. Risk controls: Discuss the risk management philosophy of the manager. How do they gauge risk? What is the fund's minimum/maximum exposure to the market? What were the highest and lowest levels of exposure for the past 12 months or since the fund's inception? Does the fund hedge against currency exposure? Interest rate exposure? What is the largest percentage of the portfolio that one single investment can represent? What is the average number of positions the fund will hold? Minimum? Maximum?

10. Operational risk: What precautions has the fund taken in case of electrical, communication, computer and software, fire, or catastrophic systems failure? Employee unavailability? Service provider unavailability? Death or injury to primary portfolio manager?

11. Leverage: Describe the fund's rationale for leverage. What are the leverage caps? (What's the maximum amount of leverage the fund will permit?) What is the average amount of leverage used? What was the highest and lowest amount of leverage used? In the past twelve months? Since the inception of the fund? Is the fund ever run without leverage? How many banks/brokers extend leverage to the fund? Has leverage ever been revoked to the fund for any reason? If so, why?

12. Taxes: Is the fund particularly advantageous for tax-exempt investors or tax-paying investors?

These are just the quantitative questions, and this is by no means an exhaustive list.

Qualitative due diligence

These questions deal specifically with the hedge fund manager and the operation.

1. Fund formation & structure: Have the manager describe the history of the organization. Who were the founders? Are they all still with the firm? If not, how/why did they leave? Are there any new principals?

2. Division of responsibility: Describe the division of power/responsibilities among the principals. Are you clear on what everyone does and why? Do the principals engage in any other activities outside management of the fund?

3. Redemption policy: Does the redemption policy of the fund match the liquidity of the investments in the fund? If so, is the redemption policy reasonable to you? Some funds will only let you redeem once a year with 60 days notice, and you have to feel comfortable with that.

4. High water mark: Does the fund have a high water mark or a high hurdle rate? Remember, we talked about this before: a hurdle rate is the minimum rate of return the manager must earn before they can charge you a performance fee. A high water mark means that performance fees don't kick in until the fund performance has surpassed their previous highest performance.

5. Conflicts of interest: Examine potential conflicts of interest (i.e. is the brokerage firm that the fund uses to execute trades also a partial owner of the hedge fund firm?)

6. Employee/principal compensation: Salaries vs. bonus breakdown. Who in the firm receives incentives?

7. Manager commitment: What percentage of the liquid net worth of the principals is invested in the fund? This is important because you want them to put their money where their mouth is. At the same time, you don't want them to put their whole net worth and mortgage their house three times over and put that all in the fund too. Why? Well, they might have a little too much on the line there. How good would their decision making be if a trade was falling apart and their whole life was on the line?

8. Manager profile: Do a full background check on the manager(s). Remember that a manager is being hired to manage capital. Go through the same motions as hiring an individual for any other profession.

9. Obtain a resume: I'm not kidding. Verify the facts of the resume such as current residence, past employers, and colleges/universities attended. (You just never know. I once hired someone who said they had an MBA but I subsequently found out they didn't. It was my fault for not checking into it. I just never thought anyone would misrepresent himself or herself to such an extent. Luckily, the damage wasn't bad, but it could've been.)

10. Obtain references: Attempt to obtain facts about their past trading history such as their past returns, volatility, and length of tenure.

11. Interviews: Interview current investors to see if they're happy with their results.

12. Personal information: What is the manager's personal life? Marital Status? Children? (I'm not kidding.) Length of time at current residence? What are his spending habits? Are they in line with his performance? Consider social issues such as the manager's physical health & fitness. Smoker? Drinker? What if the manager has a volatile ex-husband that keeps suing her in court to the point where she can't concentrate at work? Everything you just bought into with her strategy, performance, etc. can be meaningless.

13. Management team: In larger funds, there are other individuals contributing to the investment decision. Be sure to interview other key personnel as well.

14. Fund reporting: Who, if anyone, is tracking the trades? Is it in-house tracking? Or is there an outside administrator? Who is the custodian of the assets? Obtain a contact person and verify the manager's answers. Who is the prime broker? Obtain a contact person and verify the manager's answers.

15. Fund administration: This is crucial because you want to make sure the returns you're getting are the actual returns of the fund. Does the manager use a third party administrator to calculate monthly returns? If not, why? If so, find out about the fund's administrator and get the name and number for a contact at that firm. Call the contact person at the firm and ask:

16. Questions for the administrator: Are they in fact the administrator of the hedge fund? Do they calculate the value of the fund? If so, how do they calculate it? From whom do they get the data? How reliable is the data?

17. Fund auditor: You can imagine why this is so important these days. Does the manager use an auditor? If not, demand an audit — every fund should be audited annually. If the fund is new, make sure there is an auditor under contract for the end of the first year and make sure the fund has a third party calculating the monthly returns before the audit. Find out about the fund's auditor and get the name and number for a contact at that firm.

18. Questions for the auditor: How experienced are they with auditing hedge funds? Obtain names of other clients. Verify that other clients are current clients. How long have they known and worked with the fund or its manager? Have there been any problems with previous audits? If another firm performed any previous audits, call that firm and ask why the fund cancelled the relationship. Specifically, were there any problems with any of the audits they performed for that fund?

19. Fund counsel: Find out about the fund's attorneys. Ask for the name of the lawyer, the firm, the address, and their phone numbers. Is he or she willing to talk to you?

20. Comfort level: Does the manager and the fund's key administrators come across as bright, friendly, well spoken, polite, and interested in your questions? If the partnership personnel seem snobby, boastful, or secretive, it most likely indicates how the future relationship will unfold. At some point you as an investor are bound to be disappointed with a given month, or with a given quarter, or concerned in general about economic or market conditions. If the response to those concerns is not thoughtful, concerned, and forthright, you will inevitably begin to feel uncomfortable and question the relationship and the investment.

21. Transfer of assets: Never send a cheque or a wire solely in the fund's name. The fund should direct you to send your money to the prime broker, or custodial bank, "for further credit to the fund" and for further credit to an account in your name. This is true for a financial planner or advisor as well. Any manager of your money should be directing you to send the money to a larger institution. No assets should be wired or sent by cheque directly to their company.

22. Other investors: What is the profile of other investors? Individuals or institutions? Onshore vs. offshore? What is the average net worth of the investors?

23. Social fears: Don't be shy about asking questions and never be afraid to say, "No, this just doesn't feel right for me." If anything doesn't check out, get an explanation. Then confirm the explanation with additional investigation, and make sure you feel comfortable with the answers.

Source: Adapted from Due Diligence Questionnaire Channel Capital Group LLC. with the help of Michael von Mandach, Frick Capital and others.

I know that was a lot. I just want you to be aware of what is involved in this process. It's a full time job, and I don't recommend you try this at home. I'm a professional, and I don't even do this type of work without help. You can delegate this work to someone who is experienced in this area.

The more you know, the more you will invest from a position of strength and have a positive investment experience. That's what we all want. Being in the dark about anything can only lead to more risk, and a negative investment experience. There is no such thing as too much information when it comes to evaluating someone with whom you will potentially be placing a large sum of money.

Let's look at one way to pass off some of this work to people who are far more equipped to deal with this on a day to day basis: hedge fund of funds.

8

Fund of funds

As the name suggests, a fund of funds is comprised of several hedge fund strategies for the main purpose of diversification. Fund of funds, as a rule don't make direct investments, but they invest in other hedge funds. Fund of funds represent about one quarter of all hedge funds in existence, and they're growing quickly, both in numbers of funds being offered, and assets being invested.

Each fund of funds is different; it has an investment approach determined by what the other funds are that it invests in. A more diversified fund of funds can invest, for example, in 6 to 7 different strategies, and 3 managers in each strategy. Another more focused fund of funds can invest in 5 funds that are all long/short. Just because it's a fund of funds doesn't mean it's perfectly diversified among all the strategies.

You know how important it is to diversify in general. In this book we've talked about how it is important to diversify your traditional equity investments with hedge funds. Now that you know all about the different strategies that exist, and how different they all are, the next logical step in diversification would be to diversify among the different strategies in order to reduce your overall volatility of returns. Remember, just as I'm sure you've seen with mutual funds, *this year's individual hedge fund winner can be next year's loser and vice versa.* You've seen the returns of all the strategies; you've also seen the drawdowns. I'm sure you've noticed *both can be quite different at different times.*

You can diversify among the strategies yourself, but keep in mind: (1) You're going to need a pretty large portfolio to do it properly. (2) You'll have to do all the due diligence yourself. (3) You may not know which funds to invest in.

This is what a fund of funds will do for you.

Remember when we talked about correlation and how properly diversified investments have little correlation to each other? By combining investments with little or no correlation, you will reduce the overall volatility in your portfolio. Less volatility means more stable returns. More stable returns means less loss overall in your portfolio.

We talked about Mary and Bill and the returns of their portfolios on page 32. Because Bill lost money in one year, he had to make up a significant return (55%) to get to the same place as Mary, who was consistently making 15% a year. The negative effect of a loss on your portfolio is worse than the positive effect of a good return. What that means is that, mathematically, you are better off making smaller, more consistent returns than you are making larger returns, and large losses. If you lose 50% of your portfolio, and gain 50% in the next year, you're not back to where you started.

For example: $1000, with a 50% loss = $500 left. A 50% return = $750. Even though you think you're making that return back, *you're compounding on less money.* That's why, even if a technology fund that dropped by 70% and is back up 70%, many people are still under water. They made that 70% on a much smaller pool of capital than they had to start with.

I know we've already talked about this, but it's really important. The effect of less volatile returns on your portfolio is more substantial than spectacular returns and losses. *By investing in a single strategy, you take on far more risk and volatility than if you were to invest in a well-diversified fund of funds.* Investing in a diversified fund of funds that reduces the overall volatility in your portfolio will help you have more money in the bank at the end of the day.

Here's a pretty dramatic statement of a long-time investor in hedge funds and management consultant Jonathan Spring of Spring Investor Services. In his article, "Why most people should invest in fund-of-funds", he wrote:

"Unless you have at least $10 million to invest and you have plenty of time to devote to watching your managers and you have extraordinary discipline and you have a high tolerance for loss or you have more than average luck, you probably have no business investing directly in single manager funds."

We've spoken about how there are different fund of funds, some more diversified than others. If you're buying a fund of funds for diversification, you want to make sure you don't have 20 individual funds that are all exposed to the same kinds of risks and all go down at the same time. That wouldn't be very helpful, would it? A well-diversified fund of funds will have different investment styles that have *little or no correlation to each other.*

Merger arbitrage and global macro don't necessarily go up and down at the same time because they have different factors that are sources of return (and risk) for them. For example, if a merger just fell apart in the merger arbitrage fund, the global macro manager could have made quite a bit of money on a foreign exchange transaction. The two portfolio management techniques are not dependent on each other.

How many funds should you have in your fund of funds? That's an excellent question. It's excellent because the hedge fund industry does research on this all the time, and each study has a different conclusion. No one knows what the optimal number of funds is but many say between 10 and 15. Some say no more than 7 or you'll over-diversify and dilute your returns. Some say under 25 and you're taking on too much risk. You really have to evaluate each fund of funds on its own.

As we've talked about, there are many different kinds of funds of funds. (And I bet you already thought it was a jungle out there.) You have to evaluate each one on its own to see exactly how it's constructed, what risk measures the manager has in place, and how thorough their due diligence methods are.

There are some positive and negative points about fund of fund investing. We've already touched on the main benefit to fund of fund investing, and that's instant diversification of hedge fund strategies. Here are a few more benefits.

Benefits

1. Usually lower minimum investment: Because a fund of funds manager is pooling your investment capital with others to give to a manager, your minimum is much lower than if you were to try to invest with that manager directly. In the U.S., an average fund of funds has an investment minimum of $250,000 while an individual manager might have a $1 million minimum, if not higher. Trying to properly diversify your portfolio with individual hedge funds would require a substantial portfolio, several million dollars at least. With a fund of funds you have instant diversification with a much lower minimum than if you were to build a diversified portfolio yourself.

2. You may have access to funds/managers you wouldn't normally have access to: When you buy a fund of funds, you're riding on the coat tails of the relationship the fund of funds manager has with the individual managers. Some funds that are closed to new investors (remember some have a limited capacity) still remain open to fund of funds.

In addition, a good fund of funds manager can often find new talented stars before everyone else finds out about them, and before you've missed the boat. Fund of fund managers will find the best talent and then invest your funds with them. In a sense, they are like your own personal "talent scout".

3. They do all the due diligence work: That big due diligence section is covered by the fund of funds manager. All they do, all day every day, is evaluate managers and risk. They're not perfect, although I'm sure some would argue they are, and there is no guarantee that a manager they've picked won't lose money somehow. With all the background work they do, however, there is a very good chance they'll be more right than wrong before they let a manager into their fund. Having a fund of funds is like having an extra "watchdog" on your portfolio.

Here is an important point of clarification: Just because you have hired a fund of funds manager doesn't mean you can close your eyes and coast along. You still have to do your own due diligence on the fund of funds manager. But, instead of interviewing potentially 15 different managers, you can interview 2 or 3 good fund of funds managers, and pick one to do the rest of the work. We'll talk later about how you find those 2 or 3 good fund of funds managers.

4. They can overweight or underweight different strategies: A good fund of funds manager can overweight the strategies that are doing well at one particular point in the economic cycle, and underweight those that aren't doing as well. For example, if there are a lot of mergers/deals going on in the market and that particular strategy is doing very well, the fund of funds manager will overweight that strategy. On the flip side, if there aren't many bankruptcies going on in the market, and the distressed securities funds aren't doing so well, they can underweight them.

Negatives

1. Fees: (The negative we all know and love.) Yes, there are fees associated with all this due diligence work (shocking, I know) and they're not inexpensive. An average fund of funds fee might cost you about 1.5% on top of the individual manager fees in the fund. An alternative fee arrangement with the fund of funds could be a 1% flat fee and a 10% performance fee, again on top of the individual manager fees.

In my opinion you usually get what you pay for, and as I've mentioned throughout the book, I think fees are only an issue in the absence of value. If fees are a deal breaker for you, then fund of funds are not for you. I believe the price of a fund of funds is worth the time and energy it saves you in picking the best managers and keeping on top of them. Not everybody does. However, keep this in mind: paying low management fees doesn't guarantee you better returns.

2. The liquidity of the fund is driven by its individual managers: A fund of funds would be hard pressed to offer you greater liquidity for redeeming your investment than its individual managers. If the fund of funds provides you with weekly or monthly liquidity when its underlying managers do not, you should ask how they're doing that exactly. Some of the larger fund management companies are able to do this because their inflows are greater than their outflows, so they don't have to worry about redemptions. Others have to keep a cash component to meet redemptions that could put a drag on returns.

If the fund of funds is offering you frequent liquidity because they're only investing with managers that offer frequent liquidity to appeal to the masses, this is not beneficial to you. We spoke about the liquidity issue. It's natural for people to want access to their investment funds as soon as possible. But if that's the case, you may be giving up some of the better investment opportunities that may exist, as they may be less liquid.

3. You won't do as well as some of the individual managers: You probably knew this instinctively, but it's a good point to bring up. Don't be under the impression that you will perform as well as some of the "big stars" your fund of funds will likely have. Since you are diversified over several strategies, some funds will do better while some will do worse. It's the whole principle of diversification again, you won't likely hit a big home run, but you won't likely be knocked out by the ball either. Investing in a fund of funds is about managing your risk, not hitting a home run. Only you can decide if that's right for you.

4. There is no guarantee of returns in a fund of funds: Unfortunately, just because you're paying an extra fee to a fund of funds manager doesn't mean they're any good. What? Just like in every other service in life, there are the good ones that are worth their fees in gold and then there are the not-so-good ones. The not-so-good ones just go through the motions of filling in due diligence forms and doing basic interviews with managers just to say they did them.

Fund of funds performance

For the fund of funds data, I used another data provider, Channel Capital Group owners of hedgefund.net, which has the largest base of fund of funds that report to them. Because of this, the data is presented a little differently than with the individual strategies.

Let's take a look at how they've done:

Return Statistics

Year To Date:	8.87%
Highest 12 Month Return:	73.95%
Lowest 12 Month Return:	-9.84%
Average Annual Return:	15.96%
Average Monthly Return:	1.27%
Highest Monthly Return:	12.80%
Lowest Monthly Return:	-9.40%
Average Monthly Gain:	2.04%
Average Monthly Loss:	-1.20%
Compounded Monthly Return:	1.24%
Longest Losing Streak:	4 mo.
Maximum Drawdown:	-16.30%

Source: Channel Capital Group. Data as of September 30, 2003.

Year	Fund of funds Index
2003	8.87%
2002	2.26%
2001	5.07%
2000	10.32%
1999	25.03%
1998	4.27%
1997	16.94%
1996	17.74%
1995	13.18%
1994	-0.46%
1993	25.47%

Source: Channel Capital Group. Data as of September 30, 2003.

Quantitative Statistics

Sharpe Ratio (Annualized):	1.25
Std. Dev. (Monthly):	2.38%
Beta:	0.28
Alpha:	0.94

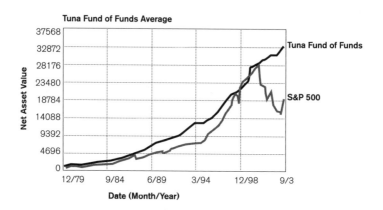

Just as we thought, the overall returns are lower than on some of the individual strategies, but the overall volatility is lower as well.

So how do you find a good fund of funds? Do your homework. Read, do research, talk to people. I've listed some great resources at the back of the book. Ask the due diligence questions of a fund of funds manager. Ask them about their due diligence process on the funds they research. I also really think getting a great financial planner or consultant that knows about hedge funds and fund of funds makes sense.

"So, you're telling me that even with a fund of funds, I still need an advisor?"

Of course it's up to you, in the end. I can only suggest what I think may make sense. Hedge funds are complicated, complex animals, so are hedge fund of funds. Having someone help you wade through all the information that's available to you, I think is a plus.

9

Hedge funds with smaller minimums

By now you may be fairly impressed with hedge funds, and may want to invest in them. But what if you don't meet the accredited investor rules? That's okay, there are ways you can invest in hedge funds through different investment vehicles that will allow you to have access to them.

By barring non-accredited investors, the securities commissions may imply that if you have less money to invest, you are less sophisticated. I think their goal is simply to protect the average investor, to the best of their ability, from losses associated with hedge fund investing. The thinking is; if you have a larger portfolio, or make a substantial amount of money on a yearly basis, you can probably sustain a loss more than someone who doesn't, can sustain a loss.

Remember, many hedge funds aren't registered, and don't have many of the same reporting or disclosure requirements as mutual funds do. The regulators have a lot less control in protecting the average consumer, you. By creating a "minimum asset test" like the accredited investor rules, at least provides some kind of safeguard. Of course, it's no guarantee that an accredited investor won't suffer a loss, but presumably his net worth will be less affected by a substantial loss.

I should clarify something here. There are two potential things impeding an investor of average net worth from investing in hedge funds: (1) The accredited investor rules. These rules don't apply if a company registers itself with the appropriate commission and issues a fully disclosed prospectus. (2) *The hedge fund company can still require a minimum investment from you to invest in their funds. That's their prerogative.* If you are accredited or not, you are still subject to the individual hedge fund account minimums that they set for their perspective clients.

Many hedge funds in the U.S. have astoundingly high minimum investment requirements because they are only interested in having a few, very high net worth clients. Some others will make the effort to do what they can to allow everyone access to their strategies. Clearly, you'll have more luck with the latter.

Things are changing to allow more people access to hedge funds, and the many benefits they can offer investors. The creation of more products and structures allow the average non-accredited investor access to hedge funds.

Let's go through some of the vehicles that exist today that allow you to invest in hedge funds without being an accredited investor. Most of these vehicles are available only in fund of funds structures, not individual strategies. As you can imagine for the guaranteed products, it's important to the guarantor that they guarantee strategies with as little volatility as possible. The guarantor is on the hook to repay the original principal back to the investor if the investment doesn't perform, so it's in their best interest to guarantee a product that has low volatility and less of a chance of under performing.

Guaranteed hedge fund linked notes

If you're nervous about the markets, this investment vehicle can potentially provide you with the best of both worlds: exposure to hedge funds as well as a principal guarantee.

A hedge fund linked note is usually guaranteed by a major bank, so it falls under the Bank Act, versus the Securities Act. A bank note is like a bank bond, or a bank guaranteed investment. For a fee, the bank agrees to guarantee your principal at the end of the term of the note. Notes usually range from 5 to 10 years. If at the end of the term of the investment, your principal value is below your initial investment the bank will make up the difference. If, on the other hand, your hedge fund made money, you get whatever the return has been over that time frame.

These "bank notes" have two basic structures. The first structure will invest about 60-70% of your funds into a bond that comes due at the end of the term; that's the guarantee covered off. Then it takes the other 30-40% of the funds and invests it into a basket of hedge funds. But if you only have $0.30 left of your dollar that's being invested, how do you make a decent return? The amount is usually leveraged and then invested.

Another version of this structure is to invest a majority of the funds in a bond, and using a call option, track the basket of hedge funds. Using an option to track the performance of the hedge funds will give you essentially the same performance as the underlying basket. In this structure you are not actually investing in the basket of hedge funds, but because of the option you are receiving essentially the same return as the basket.

The second type of structure uses something called a "dynamic hedge" to manage the risk involved of having to return your money at the end of the term. The bank puts all your money into the basket of funds right away. There is no purchase of a bond to guarantee your capital. They then monitor the performance of the basket of hedge funds on a daily basis, and take funds away from the managers if the portfolio starts to drop. They invest those funds in T-bills. When the managers start to perform again, the bank will start allocating money from T-bills to the hedge fund portfolio. As the portfolio rises more, the bank will loan the managers money (add leverage) to enhance the return. If the portfolio falls, they will remove money again.

This is also called "dynamic leverage". By constantly monitoring the returns of the portfolio and managing the fund flows accordingly, the bank manages the risk of having to fill the gap in the return at the end of the term, should you have lost money on your original investment. If things get really bad and the portfolio falls below a certain minimum threshold, the bank will redeem the fund and place it into a bond to ensure the investor's capital is guaranteed at the end of the term.

That sounds like a pretty good deal, doesn't it? Why doesn't everyone just invest this way and go to sleep for 20 years? Well, there are fees associated with this bank guarantee, usually 1-2%, between the bank and the issuer of the note (usually it's a third party that markets or distributes the note). Some people think the fees outweigh any benefit to investing this way.

I believe it depends on the product. There are some notes out there with exorbitant fees, and others with fees that are more reasonable. So, if you're going to invest in one of these notes, read the information thoroughly so you have a clear picture of what the fees are, and what you're paying for. The offering document for these guaranteed notes is an *"information statement"*, which is similar to a mutual fund prospectus.

These funds have investment minimums as low as $1000, with no accreditation requirements at all. They are offered for sale for a limited time, for example for two to three months, because the guarantee has to have a start date. The redemption periods vary, but they're usually around a week. You may have to pay fees if you redeem your fund early, and you may not get the best price. This is because the issuer might have a spread on what they're selling the share for, and what they're buying them back for. It differs from a mutual fund in this way: because there is no continuous offering of the notes, you have to sell your shares back to the issuer of the note, which is the bank. They provide you with liquidity, versus a mutual fund where there are constant purchases or redemptions.

Segregated hedge funds

These are hedge funds that are guaranteed by an insurance company. They are similar to segregated mutual funds, which you may have heard of. Segregated funds are investment vehicles that are "segregated" from the insurance company's assets, and provide insurance benefits. They provide a guarantee of principal upon death or on maturity of the term of the fund. In addition, they can provide creditor proofing, and bypass probate fees in an estate. So, this is a hedge fund with an insurance wrapper around it.

Again, there is a cost to this guarantee, usually in the 1% range. There are some guarantees that offer less than a 100% guarantee; they might offer a 75% guarantee of your principal, so they're a little less expensive. The term for the guarantee to kick in is usually 10 years, longer than a typical note structure. Some people argue that over a 10-year period, you should be able to make your principal back and think it's a waste of money to pay for a 10-year guarantee. Other disagree.

The investment minimum on the segregated funds is usually $1000. You can redeem them usually weekly, but there may be a fee associated with selling it before the maturity date.

Commodity/futures pool funds

There are some managed futures funds that register themselves and offer a full prospectus, in the same way a mutual fund would. Because of the registration and full prospectus disclosure, the accredited investor rules don't apply, and they are available to the general public. Investing in a managed futures fund is very similar to investing in a mutual fund in terms of the investment minimum being lower (usually $5000), daily liquidity, full transparency, etc. There are funds that look and feel like managed futures funds from a regulatory requirement perspective but are actually far more versatile in their portfolio management techniques. Don't forget, where once you could only buy futures on commodities, you can now buy futures on many other things like stock indexes, currencies, and bonds.

Closed-end hedge fund trusts

A closed-end hedge fund is a hedge fund that trades on an exchange, just as a stock would. These vehicles are filed with the securities regulators and have a full prospectus. A closed-end fund is issued in the same way a "new issue" for a stock is issued. There are underwriters (banks/brokerages) who can offer the fund for sale to their clients through their investment advisor distribution network. The closed-end fund is made available for sale for a limited offering period, usually two to three months, at which point it is closed off to new investors.

Liquidity is an issue with closed-end trusts. Because it trades on an exchange as a stock would, in order to sell your shares you have to find a buyer for them. Remember, it's not as widely traded as a blue chip stock. It's usually a smaller offering, so they don't issue as many shares as a regular company would if it was going public.

If you want to sell your trust you have to find a buyer for it. In addition to that, your shares may trade at a discount to their actual net asset value on the exchange. If you can wait, the trust will usually have an offer to buy back your shares once a year at the net asset value. The net asset value is the true value of the assets in the trust, which can be different than the market value on an exchange.

Because this type of offering is offered under a full prospectus and registered with the securities regulators you don't have to be an accredited investor. Investment minimums are usually around $2000.

Hedge funds "light"— mutual fund hedge funds

What are these you may ask? These are hedge funds that file a full prospectus with the various regulators, but aren't real mutual funds in the traditional sense of the word. This is like a quasi-mixed hedge fund product with mutual fund characteristics. They don't have all the restrictions of mutual funds, nor do they have all the freedom of hedge funds.

For cxample, you can still short-sell, use leverage and derivatives in a registered investment fund (mutual fund) in many cases but only to a limited extent. (In Canada, you can't unless you get special regulatory relief.)

So there is a small group of "mutual fund light funds" that offer hedge fund strategies within the context of the restrictions placed on them. It is usually large mutual fund companies that include this type of fund as part of their overall offering of funds. They are not called hedge funds because they fall under the mutual fund banner, but they will have names such as, ABC Market-Neutral fund or, XYZ Long/Short fund.

I call these hedge fund "light" strategies because they do offer many of the same strategies we spoke about. But they have tighter restrictions on the techniques they can use, and to what extent. For example, some of these registered funds are allowed to hold no more than 15% of their assets in illiquid investments, whereas a hedge fund can hold 100% of their assets in illiquid investments if they thought it made sense. They are permitted to short-sell provided they place funds aside to cover their short position. This ties up investment funds, as collateral would on a loan. Hedge funds aren't restricted in this way.

One of the nice things about hedge fund "light" products is that they have many of the positive benefits of mutual funds. Aside from the low investment minimum of $1000 or so, they offer daily liquidity and pricing, as well as full transparency and reporting.

Registered hedge fund of funds

More and more funds of hedge funds in the U.S. are registering themselves with the SEC and are registering the offering of their securities for sale under the Securities Act. In other words, they are using prospectuses to offer investments to the general public. This is great news. (This hasn't happened in Canada yet.)

We spoke about the great diversification funds of funds provide, but only to accredited investors. To invest in a registered fund of funds that registers its securities for sale under the Securities Act, means you don't have to be an accredited investor. By being registered in this way and issuing a prospectus, they can offer their securities for sale to the general public. Many of these funds still have their own minimums for investment, but they may be lower than the unregistered fund of funds. The only caveat is you have to find the ones that are registered.

The regulators are thinking about this issue as well. In the September 2003 SEC report, "Implications of the Growth of Hedge Funds", here was one of the recommendations made: "The commission should consider issuing a concept release for wider use of hedge fund investment strategies in registered investment companies." They go on to state, "We believe it may be the case that retail investors interested in absolute return strategies should be able to pursue those investments through the registered investment company structure." The full report is available online at the SEC website.

The more interest there is from average investors who don't meet the accreditation test, the more the regulators will be forced to further examine the issues around the current regulations. Remember, the regulator's job is to protect the investor from potential harm. Hopefully, the more educated investors become about the risks and rewards of hedge funds, the more the regulations will reflect that new education.

The investment vehicles available today for the non-accredited investor aren't perfect. Some are better structured than others are. Some have more fees and some have less, depending on the specifics of the product. In general, they provide a good way for investors to have access to an asset class that provides great diversification, and potentially reduces the overall risk in their portfolio.

Do the benefits of being in these types of hedge fund structures outweigh the potentially higher fees associated with these products? In my opinion, they do. That said, you must still do your homework on these products to fully understand how they work and what fees are associated with them. Only then can you make a proper decision as to whether any of them make sense for you, given your personal circumstances.

10

How to incorporate hedge funds into your portfolio

I hope that by this point you see many of the benefits of investing in hedge funds. You may be so impressed with them that you may think; "I want to put my whole portfolio in hedge funds!" Well, I would go slowly first until you get comfortable, then increase your allocation as time goes on. Don't jump into this like it's the latest, greatest thing. If this is going to be a long-term relationship between you and hedge funds, you don't need to run to Las Vegas and get married by Elvis on the first night. Take it slowly, test the waters, and go in with your eyes wide open. We've talked about the importance of risks, and understanding them fully before you invest. Dip your toe in first. You'll be grateful you did.

So you're looking at your portfolio right now and thinking; "Okay, I want to add some hedge funds to my portfolio, where should I put them? How much should I allocate? Should I sell something or just contribute new funds? How many funds should I buy? Which ones? When do I sell them?"

What do you think I'm going to answer? *It depends.* Are you 25 or 75 years old? Are you conservative or a big risk taker? How big is your portfolio? What's your previous investment experience? How much time do you like to spend monitoring your investments? These are just a few of the questions you need to ask yourself that I can't answer for you.

You can invest by yourself, but I'm warning you again, there is a whole lot of work involved.

If you don't have the time, resources and energy to devote to the investment process, then *hire someone* to help you. You may already have someone and that's wonderful. Maybe they even gave you this book so you could learn more about hedge funds. Having an advisor is, in my humble opinion, the better route. I believe you need a really good financial advisor/broker who knows what they're talking about when it comes to hedge funds.

Think of all the things in your life you outsource right now. Do you have someone who fixes your car for you? What about an assistant or secretary at work? Does the dry cleaner clean your clothes? Do you have an accountant or a lawyer? Out of all the things in your life that you pay someone to do for you, what could be more important than the person who is helping you manage your money?

"But," you say to me, "you've got to give me some clue as to at least how much exposure to hedge funds you think I should have." Nope. I won't even tell you that academic studies show you should have X amount, because academic studies are just that, studies. They have no idea of the size of your portfolio, how old you are, or your current situation. They don't know who you are or where you've been in your investment life, and more importantly, they have no idea where you'd like to go. That's what your planner/advisor/consultant is there for.

Everybody has a different personal and financial situation. Aside from the due diligence work, which is extremely important, a good financial planner or consultant will help you to choose the fund or funds that are most appropriate for you.

In the end, you have to feel comfortable with your investments. After all, you may lose money. A good financial planner or advisor will work with you to help you find not only what you're looking for (or, what you think you're looking for) but what you're most comfortable with, based on your own personal circumstances, and your own personal tolerance for loss or volatility in your portfolio.

If you don't have one, how do you find a good advisor who knows about hedge funds? In the U.S. there are many *hedge fund consultants* that specialize in this area. They will provide due diligence services, analyze different offerings, and assist in the monitoring of your investments. Some of them might manage their own hedge funds as well, so that may present some conflicts of interest. In addition, some of them might have high investment minimums.

There are also *financial planners* who work for a fee. Many of them are knowledgeable in this area. There are some well-known financial planning firms that you can go to, and ask them to refer you to someone who is knowledgeable and experienced with hedge funds.

If you are in Canada, you can go to my website for a listing of advisors that I know who are knowledgeable in the hedge fund area: *www.hedgefundlady.com*

There are a lot of financial advisors out there, but not all of them even know about hedge funds or are knowledgeable enough to invest in them. Please be careful. Here are some questions you might ask a potential advisor:

- How long have they been an advisor? What's their background?
- How long have they been advising clients on hedge funds?
- What is their educational background on hedge funds? Have they read any books? Taken any courses? Do they have any kind of formal training in this area?
- Who are their other clients that invest in hedge funds? Are they like you? Can you talk to any of them about their experience with this advisor?
- Do they have hedge fund support from the firm they work for? Is there a research analyst covering hedge funds and doing all the due diligence, or do they do it all themselves? Remember, that was a fairly big list of due diligence questions, does the advisor have help answering them all?
- Do they themselves invest in hedge funds?

After you have found out that they have the knowledge and the prerequisite skills necessary, I think the most important thing is that *you feel comfortable with them.*

If you received this book from your advisor or your broker, then kudos to you as you are probably already working with someone who is knowledgeable in the field. Giving you this book shows that they want to help you to you understand this very important asset class for your ultimate benefit.

Now, let's talk to some people who have incorporated hedge funds into their portfolios…

11

Straight from the horse's mouth: Interviews with hedge fund investors

"Experience will guide us to the rules...
You cannot make rules precede practical experience."
– Antoine de Saint-Exupéry

To complete your hedge fund learning curve, it is really important to include some interviews with people who have invested in hedge funds. There is a lot to learn in speaking to current and past hedge fund investors. Only then will you have a true feel for what you can expect, the good and the bad.

The people I selected to interview are a random sample that come from different backgrounds: some are older, some are younger, some retired, some executives, some business owners. Some happy, some not as happy with their hedge fund experiences.

These are individuals who are all currently invested in various types of hedge funds. All are accredited investors with the exception of two. They are also all Canadian. This is of course not a statistically valid survey, it's a Hedge Fund Lady general interest survey. In addition, not every interviewee answered every question.

The following people participated. Below you will see their names, ages, occupations, and current allocation to hedge funds. Throughout the interviews, you will see their first name only and their responses to a series of questions about their hedge fund experience.

Participant	Age	Occupation	Allocation
Bill*	65	Retired	30%
Jack Bowman	76	Retired	<10%
Mohamed Ladha	28	Management & IT consultant	15-20%
Hendrik Weiler	65	Retired (currently in France)	25%
Dr.Joel Weiss	63	Retired Professor Senior Fellow University of Toronto	33%
Anthony Tersigni	38	Business Owner	80%
Carrie*	32	Senior Commercial Bank Manager	25%
Jack Fleishman	49	Systems Technology Analyst	30%
Roger*	63	Retired	30%
Michael F. Boyce	39	Director of Corporate/ Business Development GoodLife Fitness Clubs Inc.	20%
Richard*	58	Retired	10-20%
Cole Jordan	38	President, Software Company	20%
Peter Jansen	46	IT Consultant	30%
Mark Stein	36	Owner of Marketing Agency	80%

(* last name withheld by request)

Questions

How many years have you been investing and in what vehicles ?

In summary, people have invested from 10-30 years depending on their age. Most started off in either mutual funds or guaranteed investments. Some moved on to invest in stocks, others remained in mutual funds. Essentially all traditional vehicles, stocks, bonds, mutual funds, GICs, etc. until they invested in hedge funds.

What portion of your portfolio is dedicated to hedge funds?

I've divided the allocation up into three basic categories that encompass all the interviewees. Two investors had an 80% allocation to hedge funds (they are included in the 30%+ category).

Allocation to hedge funds	10-15%	20-25%	30% or more
# of people	2	5	7

How did you first find out about hedge funds?

Most investors found out about hedge funds through their financial planner/advisor. Some had read about them in the press.

Did you have any concerns before investing in hedge funds?

Most people didn't have concerns once it was fully explained to them by their planner/advisor, and they knew what to expect. Those who did have concerns, or particular remarks are listed below:

Jack B: I didn't really understand them at first. I was a little apprehensive at first, and quite frankly still am. They haven't really done what I expected, even though we haven't lost any money, we really haven't made any either.

Mohamed: My only concern was, if next year, the guy next to me makes a 20% return, am I going to make that same return? I'm not concerned if the market drops 20%, I know I'm safe. Even though I knew about them, they were sort of a mythical tool that big players used. I had more questions, than concerns.

Anthony: I was a little bit hesitant; you get that offering memorandum in the mail, it's a little intimidating. I have an accounting background so I can understand most of the things they're trying to say. I can imagine if you don't know anything about it, it might be intimidating.

Carrie: I think everybody who reads the press has heard all the horror stories about hedge funds, Long-Term Capital Management and that implosion… in terms in of getting a genuine view of hedge funds, it was my current advisor who has been following hedge funds for a number of years who helped me.

I think hedge funds are a legitimate investment strategy at any point in the economic cycle, but now you're hearing about it constantly in the press because of the volatility in the markets, like it's a fad, which is really not the case.

Jack F: I was under the impression that hedge funds were very risky. I read about them in 1998, when Long-Term Capital Management had to be bailed out by the U.S. government. It seemed it wasn't something for the average guy like me; I didn't even invest in individual stocks, only mutual funds.

But the more I read, and spoke to my advisor, the more I realized the primary idea of hedge funds was to reduce volatility, not to increase it. That's what caught my attention; because like everybody else I suffered during the dark days of 2001-2002 when everything went down the drain.

One thing that comforted me was that a lot of large institutions use hedge funds significantly, primarily because they want to reduce volatility as much as possible.

Michael: It took me 12-24 months to invest from the time I found out about them, and part of the longer wait time was because the advisor I was with previously didn't know about them. He wasn't someone who was educated on them like my current advisor is. This was part of the reason for changing advisors. Other than that, I was very comfortable once I had the right advisor. I had no real concerns before investing.

Cole: I was careful. I seeded an initial investment (1-2%) to watch it for six months and it performed really well during that time, and then I went in a lot bigger. Two concerns, at that point it was a new advisor, and hedge funds were new, but a friend of mine had already invested in hedge funds so that was a mitigating factor. I knew someone who was prospering because of hedge funds.

Mark: I was a little skeptical at first. Hedge funds to me initially had the issue of risk attached to them, and I didn't feel I was in a position to be risky.

As I understood they were always a vehicle for the rich, and it always seemed to be just for that portion of the portfolio they could have at risk. Not being a wealthy person, I wanted to have my money protected. I had to feel comfortable that my advisor knew the manager was a quality manager, and that was scary for me at first.

What was it that made it so attractive to you to want to invest in these strategies?

Bill: What attracted me was the potential for increased returns coupled with reduced risk; a strategy that can take advantage of all market conditions.

Jack B: Safety was the attraction for me. For me, it was about managing risk. I'm told we can have a real market crash, and that's the feature that keeps me in hedge funds, the "just-in-case" feature.

Mohamed: Hedge funds were (and still are) all about risk management. That was the attraction to me.

Hendrik: I could make money if the markets went up- or went down. Mutual funds only make money if the markets go up.

Joel: I previously thought that hedge funds were by and large for people who were quite wealthy, and we didn't fit into that category. If you understood what you are doing, and chose wisely, hedge funds are in many ways actually a very conservative way of investing.

Particularly with the volatility of markets, it is possible to have a virtually zero correlation with what markets are doing. Since we had not done very well investing in the traditional investments, given the swings in the market, that factor made them very attractive to us.

The compensation structure of the managers was attractive to me as well, the fact that they get paid on how successful they are made sense, versus getting a flat fee regardless of how well they do.

Anthony: I was just tired of negative returns. The market was in a steady decline, and it didn't look like it would turn around, and hedge funds seemed like an alternative we could explore.

Carrie: It's difficult for the average investor to make money in the markets and I think it's important to have a protection strategy in there. I wanted preservation of capital, and I think maybe we all got caught off guard when things we thought were "blue-chip" suddenly went down 80%; that's not acceptable, in anyone's portfolio, that's a lot of money to have to earn back over the years.

I think there are a few, incredibly skilled people in understanding the markets, and knowing what to do to consistently make investors' money. Most of those people are in the hedge fund industry. I'm a lot more comfortable dealing with people who I think have some skill. To be frank, my opinion of mutual funds is that they're lemmings, and they just follow the index so you get index returns, less a 2% management fee. Unless there's some "specialty"unique characteristic of a fund, I don't see why anyone would want to be in a regular equity mutual fund. I don't see any value there at all.

Ultimately, I think you can get to the same place, it's just how you can get there. You can get similar or better returns with hedge funds over time (versus traditional investments) without having to take on all the risk and volatility.

Jack F: What attracted me was the volatility component, the fact that they're "real returns". They don't really move in accordance with the market, they seem to go up in a straight line. Some months are better than others, but they're unrelated to what the market does. That's really important to me. I wish I would have invested in them sooner.

Roger: I was attracted by better returns, especially in a down market. Also, I think the managers have better incentive to perform because of the compensation structure.

Michael: Because most of my portfolio is in equities/cash, there's certainly a higher level of risk there, which I wanted to reduce. The cost to getting involved in hedge funds seemed very reasonable; the manager took a higher fee only when they had exceptional performance. This seemed to be more in line with traditional business sense where if you do well, you are compensated for it. I saw it as a real selling feature because you're not paying the same fee whether you win or lose.

Richard: The reported returns were the inducement. When mutual funds were down, the hedge funds still seemed to be in double digits. Having the potential for returns in any market.

Cole: Two things attracted me to hedge funds; first the concept of an "absolute return", that in any market it should make money. Second, that a hedge fund isn't tied to a particular index. With a mutual fund, if an index goes down by 30%, and a mutual fund goes down by 29% we should all be happy. That type of benchmark doesn't get me excited by any means.

The concept also that it could get out of the market when the market goes down or goes sideways and can go to cash. The fact that they don't get paid to be fully invested, they get paid to make money, that concept was quite appealing.

Peter: I held a very undiversified portfolio of technology stocks through the nineties, and did very well. You just couldn't miss. You throw a dart, you have a winner. I think that's what people expected the norm to be. So when the whole bubble burst, you thought it was going to come back. Well it's not coming back, and I didn't need a fund that was tied to the index, that meant nothing to me.

Hedge funds were an alternative. Based on the performance, they had a history of doing well regardless of market conditions. So, the attraction of the track record was one.

The second thing that attracted me was, as an alternative investment strategy, they weren't simply tying themselves to the index, they were doing different things to try to get better yields for their investors.

The fact that the larger pension funds were involved in this, and this was a sophisticated investment strategy used by those who do this for a living, gave me a lot of comfort. And the fact that investment managers themselves have to put a certain percentage of their own capital in. I'm also a firm believer in paying for performance.

Mark: Essentially, it was because the market made it difficult for me to make money, in fact I lost money in the market, along with everyone. I had more comfort in the ability of an individual. The fact that hedge funds were independent of the market was something that I liked. The market downturn really turned my focus onto hedge funds.

What strategies are you invested in? Overall how have they done?

Below is a summary of responses. The majority of interviewees were up or flat.

Up	Down	Flat	Not Sure
7	1	5	1

Selected comments:

Hendrik: A combination of different strategies. Both of my investments have made a minimum of 150% within 2-4 years.

Anthony: Long/short, a couple of fund of funds. About 12% overall, since I've had them (2 years).

Roger: Fund of funds, market neutral, long/short. Overall, very well. I don't know exactly, but one is up 30% over the past four years.

Michael: Fund of funds, investing for 2 years; we've definitely seen growth, high single digits.

Richard: Fund of funds, a note, for about 2 years, but they've been flat.

Cole: At this point, I'm mostly in fund of funds. I've been in individual strategies like long/short, and market neutral, but I got out of them, they were too volatile. As individual strategies, they were too correlated to the market.

Mark: Mostly fund of funds; one fund is slightly more conservative, the other slightly more aggressive. The aggressive one has been fabulous, up 30% year to date since January 2003. The more conservative one is meeting its target of 8-10% a year.

Do you think your portfolio return/risk profile has improved since adding hedge funds to the mix?

Below is a summary of the answers:

Yes	No	Not Sure (too soon to tell)
8	2	4

Selected comments:

Jack B: I think they should have done more, but I'm happy to leave them and see what happens.

Hendrik: The major contributions to my portfolio's positive returns have been made with hedge funds.

Mohamed: The risk has absolutely improved, there's no question about it. I think people don't understand the importance of risk management in their portfolios and the benefits that hedge funds bring to that risk management.

I'm getting what I wanted out of them, and compared to the beating the rest of my portfolio took over the not too distant past, it's stellar, absolutely stellar. The last couple of years, has tempered one's beliefs; during the glory days, everybody wins, but when the glory days are over, you have to manage risk if you want your money to work for you.

Joel: It's hard to say if my risk/return improved. But as unsophisticated as I was, I realized the advice we were getting previously with our last advisor was not appropriate for people of our age. We were too heavily exposed to the market, in too high risk a position, and there was a problem.

Anthony: My risk/return profile has absolutely improved. Before I switched into hedge funds from stocks/mutual funds, I was down 40% from the high. Now, I've managed to make some of that back, which I think is outstanding, compared to other people that I talk to, who are still down even further.

Carrie: Yes, my risk/return profile has improved. It's nice to have an asset that is skill-based, and not just market-based. I don't know what's going on in the market these days; it really bothers me, there's no rhyme or reason to it. You see tech funds/stocks going sky high with no earnings. As long as there is no reason behind it, I'm not comfortable having my whole portfolio exposed to the market, as opposed to hedged.

Michael: Yes, I think my risk has improved. Hedge funds are for me a more stable vehicle; there's more risk in the other parts of my portfolio.

Richard: The returns haven't improved. The risk? It dampened it down. They haven't really provided the return that one was expecting from what was advertised. There seems to be a difference in returns between the regular hedge funds and the fund of fund notes, but I don't have access to the regular ones as a common (non-accredited) investor.

But I haven't lost money and in actuality, I invested in those in a bear market, so in many cases I actually made money. It's the two sides of the coin, but that wasn't my goal. I didn't get in because they were advertising flat returns in a bear market.

Cole: I would say my risk/return profile has not really improved. The funds I originally invested in were too correlated to the market, they were really long only disguised. The fund of funds that I have now brings value, because it is really hedged. But there are many that don't practice what they preach.

In all honesty, the fund of funds have done what they said they would. A fund of funds has a much better chance of achieving its goals than a single strategy.

I want them to meet their expectations. Over 3 years, I have made about 1.4% a year. At the worst possible time in the market with hedge funds, I was down about 12%, which overall, was pretty darned good. This year alone we're up 8% or 9%, so we're back in the black.

Mark: The question "has your risk/return profile improved since adding hedge funds to your portfolio" is a technical way of describing that I feel more comfortable. In terms of risk/reward, even when the market killed me, it still fit my risk profile. I feel that my money is better protected now. I feel better; I never question my risk/reward profile. When you are younger, you tend to go more for home runs, obviously that strategy didn't work.

Do you plan on increasing your allocation to Hedge funds in the future?

Yes	No	Maybe
5	4	5

Bill: Maybe,(from 30%) if I find one I really like; one that offers safety and cash flow.

Mohamed: Yes, I am going to take it to 50% (from 15-20%). I haven't really found a good answer as to what amount should be in hedge funds. Theory says if you're looking at an absolute return paradigm it should be about all of your portfolio. I'm not sure I'm entirely there yet, I'm still waiting for things to play out a bit before I'm willing to take that step.

Hendrik: Possibly (from 25%). I am a non-resident of Canada now, and am looking for wider diversification than simply North America. Hence hedge funds make sense if they are diversified outside North America. Otherwise, no.

Joel: (from 33%) If I had any large sums of money coming in (which I don't anticipate unless I win the lottery) or unless my advisor wanted to do some re-allocation, I don't anticipate a large move, but if it makes sense, and my advisor recommends it, then maybe.

Anthony: Yes (from 80%). Most of my new investment funds are going to hedge funds.

Carrie: Yes definitely, I'd like to increase it pretty dramatically over the medium term (from 25%).

Jack F: I don't think so, I think 30% is probably a significant percentage already.

Roger: Possibly to 40% (from 30%).

Michael: I don't think so. My advisor and I have had discussions about it, and we think 20% is the benchmark for now.

Richard: At this point, no (from 10-20%). I'm waiting to see what kind of returns the fund of fund notes will have

Cole: I'm not sure (from 20%). I keep looking for funds that meet their expectations, hedge or not. I'm more partial to hedge, because they have more strategies for getting there. I think hedge has more opportunities to deliver on expectations rather than relying on the market and long only mutual funds.

Peter: In the very near future, I would say no (from 30%) because the equities are picking up a bit, and I'd like to see how the hedge funds I have do over the next six months or so. I can't predict past that, we'll have to see how they perform.

Mark: (from 80%) I plan on increasing that allocation; I plan on putting quite a bit more money into hedge funds.

How do you feel about traditional vehicles now? (stocks, bonds, etc.)

Mohamed: Traditional vehicles still have a place in my portfolio right now. It's the devil I know, I understand how that industry works, I understand the regulation mechanisms that are in place. There's a level of transparency (or at least supposed to be) a level of transparency I'm comfortable with.

I'd like a better handle on the regulatory environment of hedge funds. I don't have a clear understanding of that yet, except for the guaranteed products. If I get the level of comfort, and understand how the regulatory environment works, I'd be willing to take my portfolio to a 50% allocation in hedge funds.

Hendrik: I'm neutral on traditional investments. If they make money, fine. My philosophy is that "there is always another bus."

Joel: Hedge funds were necessary in my situation to help balance our portfolio. I'm moving more away from individual stocks. It depends on the economic picture, what my advisor recommends, and what seems to be appropriate at the time.

Anthony: I think traditional vehicles are great, if you know what you're doing. I usually don't to tell you the truth. I made some money on individual stocks, but I think it's just pure luck, like many people at the time. Hedge funds have been working: the market's been down, and they're still up.

Carrie: I'm fairly unimpressed with traditional vehicles. I don't like your average mutual fund. Trying to make investment decisions based on historical returns is what almost all mutual fund/ stock pickers do, and I don't think it works very well anymore. It's a bit of a crap-shoot as to whether you win or lose now when you're buying stocks.

Jack F: I still feel you have to participate in traditional vehicles as well, you have to be exposed to the market, there's a role to play. The hedge funds are there to reduce the volatility of your portfolio.

Roger: Traditional vehicles, hedge funds, they all have their place. It all depends on the investor and their advisor's experience and knowledge. You really want a good advisor.

Michael: I still have a large portion of my portfolio in traditional vehicles. I view hedge funds as stability; you can benefit on the way up and on the way down, it's a comfort level in the portfolio knowing there's that constant return; there's very little negativity in the hedge fund portion of the portfolio. I still try to take advantage of a particular stock, or any other vehicle that might benefit us.

Cole: I think I've actually learned to like traditional vehicles more, actually. Having been in hedge funds for three years, I see now they have a place in a portfolio, but they're not just the be-all and end-all. I expect my advisor to not be focused on one strategy, to be focused on multiple strategies and go where the market is going. It's obvious that hedge funds can't be up all the time.

Peter: Traditional vehicles, well, there's no way I would want to put 100% of my portfolio into any one instrument. I think there needs to be a good balance between them; I think there's still a large role for traditional equity markets.

Mark: I think traditional vehicles have their place, but I would invest in them differently now. Hedge funds are a good answer for a guy my age (36) who wants to participate in equity-type investments. I think they're a good alternative to equities.

Any negative comments or thoughts about hedge funds or your experience?

Bill: My negative experience came when I invested in a hedge fund that used option strategies. When 9/11 came, it caused a big hit to the fund because many of the options were exercised, something the manager wasn't counting on. I took a big hit, I don't know how much exactly. I should've trusted my own gut feeling and gotten out when I thought, instead of hanging on and hoping.

Mohamed: No negative experiences for me personally. If you're the kind of person that likes to move your money around, I can see why you might see that as a disadvantage, because they're not as liquid as traditional vehicles. But that's not the case for me. I don't see anything wrong with that. I don't have full transparency, and it's a bit of double-edged sword, because once that information becomes public knowledge, I've missed the boat.

Hendrik: No negative comments at this stage. They have made significant money for me. The key is to bail out once they start to falter or non-perform.

Joel: No, we're only been in for just over 1 year, so maybe I don't have enough experience yet.

Anthony: None so far.

Carrie: No negative experiences, but I think you do have to be cautious, and you need a broker who is very conscientious because it requires a lot of due diligence.

Jack F: You can't see the value of your fund easily because they're only priced once a month. It's not as easily accessible as a mutual fund, it's not easy to see how well they're doing. They are pretty technical, all the strategies that the hedge fund managers are pursuing. For the average person, it's difficult to understand exactly what they're doing. With mutual funds, it's pretty easy to understand.

Roger: Transparency is atrocious. In my opinion, hedge funds should be as transparent as mutual funds are now. I'm assuming that mutual funds will be more transparent in the future but do not expect that much transparency from hedge funds. Investors are often at a disadvantage; you can't see the information you need to make a decision.

Roger: Many hedge funds are going offshore, and many laws don't apply there. That's a serious risk. Another thing that bothers me is there doesn't seem to be any standard set of groupings for different hedge fund styles; they're all defined differently depending on where you look.

Michael: No, I don't think there's anything really negative about them, other than the fact it took me switching advisors to clarify the benefits to an investor like myself. A lack of education or a lack of information on hedge funds might be the only negative.

Richard: The major issue for me is the price of get in, the accreditation rules. With the notes, you can enter them without being accredited, but I don't think they've performed as well as the regular hedge funds; the management cost seems too expensive in a fund of funds note.

Cole: The issue of "absolute returns" all the time is just not the case. The hedge funds I invested in originally (individual strategies) did lose money.

Peter: Clearly, I'm a little disappointed that my first few months we haven't seen some fantastic returns that would make me feel "Wow, that's the right thing". But by the same token, we should try to take a little bit of a long term view with it, and see where it goes.

Mark: My experience has been favorable. The market was something not in my control. Choosing a hedge fund manager feels more within my control. The negative piece is, there is less diffusion of responsibility. When the market "crashed" it did provide me with a certain amount of comfort that at least I wasn't the only person who lost a lot of money. In hedge funds, I'm relying on my advisor, and I'm relying on my advisor choosing another individual. It feels like I own the problem a little bit more as opposed to the "market", which I have no control over.

What advice would you give other investors who are considering hedge funds?

Bill: Don't be too greedy, take some profits along the way. You have to do your homework. You have to understand the philosophy /strategy of the manager and what they're doing. You have to learn to lose, you can't win all the time; you should win most of the time. Nobody can predict the market, you've got to pick the best fund, and see what it does in a good market, and in a bad market.

Mohamed: I would say, before you consider hedge funds, look at what your goals are and understand how risk fits into your overall financial picture. Understand that, yes returns are important, but risk is even more important than the return, because protecting the capital that you have is not worth the risk of diminishing that capital.

Once you understand how important it is to reduce your risk, you can look at different ways of doing that. You will not find a better mechanism that will allow you to reduce your risk, while giving you some very decent returns, than a hedge fund. You simply cannot find a better balance.

Hendrik: Consider hedge funds seriously, since this is the only vehicle (aside from personal long/short buying/selling) that allows you to take advantage of market rises, as well as falls. But check out the managers of the funds and their history!

Joel: It's very important to have faith in your adviser. Hedge funds are a sophisticated instrument most people probably should not be involved with unless they have a trusted advisor who really understands hedge funds. My advice would be to have somebody that has demonstrated to you that they understand hedge funds, and have experience using them. Be worried about going to a "Johnny come lately" advisor who doesn't have a track record with hedge funds.

We've seen the highs, we've seen the lows, and we've become sophisticated enough to say that we have to be careful about trying to follow "the yellow brick road". We have to understand that there may well be some things that outperform hedge funds at certain times, but on the whole, we'll probably do at least as well or better in hedge funds, and it will take some of the volatility out. The market has not been that good since I've retired, but I've really been pleased with how our hedge funds have worked out.

Anthony: I highly promote them. I'm a disciple, I really believe in them. I really think they work. Now's the time to get in, while we're still on the ground floor. I see more of the larger fund companies are developing their own hedge fund products. It's going to become more mainstream soon.

Carrie: I would definitely recommend them, to those I thought were reasonably sophisticated investors. I would be a lot more careful about recommending an advisor to make sure that any hedge fund investment they did would be thoroughly researched. That, to me, is the most important thing of all, to work with someone that is qualified and knowledgeable about hedge funds because not all advisors are. I wouldn't recommend a specific hedge fund, I would recommend they speak to an expert on hedge funds.

Jack F: It should be seriously considered primarily as a vehicle to reduce volatility. Never buy individual strategies, stick with the fund of funds. This is a full-time job, looking at them, trying to figure which ones are better than others, what it is they're doing. I wouldn't do it on my own, I would much rather leave this to a professional to worry about. You don't go to an optometrist with a foot problem; go to someone who specializes in this area.

Roger: Get a very good advisor and/or do one heck of a lot of research yourself.

Michael: If I'd offer the advice to my parents, I would certainly tell them to have a higher percentage of hedge funds in their portfolio. I think when you're 39 years old like I am, you can take on a little bit more risk in your portfolio, which means that your percentage of hedge funds in your portfolio is going to be lower.

Also, have somebody that you can use, that you feel comfortable with, that you trust and that will give you the information that you need so that you can make the best decisions, because ultimately it's up to the individual investor. If people have the opportunity, take advantage of somebody who does this for a living. You can't be a master of everything. My advice is to take advantage of other people's skills and talents.

Richard: Be cautious about returns that are being offered by these multi-manager hedge funds. I'm not familiar with all of them, of course, I've only had the experience with one or two.

Cole: I would say they can still be risky, and not to have more than 10-20% of your portfolio in them. It's probably all you really need. The other thing I would say is getting the right advisor is really important because transparency in hedge funds is pretty difficult. There's not a lot of information, there's not a lot of government intervention, and there's a lot more money involved. Having an advisor that drills down is huge. With my advisor, we set a maximum draw-down limit for every hedge fund we invested in.

Peter: I would advise people to look at them. I would advise people to seek out somebody who knows enough about them to make the right choices. Because it's like anything, there's always winners, and there's always losers. I can't believe anything is fail safe. It represents an interesting and attractive alternative for a portion of a portfolio.

Mark: Make sure you understand them completely. First and foremost, understand the integrity and value system of the individual who is providing you with this advice, your financial planner/advisor. You have to be comfortable with them.

Closing thoughts
from the
Hedge Fund Lady

Well, here we are, the end of the book. I wish I had a crystal ball to tell you which way the market will move. You know I don't, and I hope that you also know by now that no matter what the market does going forward, is moot. The incredible volatility of the traditional markets has shown us that they are impossible to predict. Add to that the scandals in corporate America over the last couple of years, and the market becomes a monstrous, erratic beast. It's a beast that can create havoc in your investment portfolio if you let it.

You can't invest the way you used to anymore. Things are different. To be fully exposed to the market, in its current state, is like playing roulette with your investments. Maybe the market will change; maybe it will go back to becoming more predictable, and follow a constant upward trend like it did throughout the 1990's. Let's hope so. But until then, let's be proactive about diversifying away from the traditional market.

I trust you now see that hedge funds, with all their different strategies and techniques, can provide you with some of that diversification. As a group, they are also far less volatile than long only strategies and over time, have performed better in many respects.

I hope that I have dispelled some of the myths you may have heard about hedge funds, but at the same time, taught you caution as you go forward on your journey. The risks are certainly inherent if you don't do your homework, so please do.

You have read interviews with people and their experiences with hedge fund investing. This has hopefully given you a true feel for investing in this asset class if you're new to it, or a different perspective to your own experience if you're already an investor.

Hedge fund investing, from both institutions and individuals, is growing more quickly than investments into any other asset class. Maybe the perils of investing in the traditional markets has forced people into looking at alternatives. Perhaps they could no longer deny the irrefutable evidence that investing in hedge funds presents. Whatever the reason, people are experiencing first hand how much value this asset class can add to their portfolios.

If you have an experience you'd like to share, write me an email. I'd love to hear from you. Maybe I will be speaking in your city sometime in the near future, and you can tell me in person.

In the meantime, I wish you the very best of success going forward. Invest wisely. Be cautious. Find a great person to help you on your journey. You'll be just fine.

Sincerely,

Renata Neufeld
www.hedgefundlady.com

Resources

If you would like to read more about Hedge Funds, the following books and websites are excellent:

Absolute Returns by Alexander M. Ineichen
Managing Risk in Alternative Investment Strategies by Lars Jaeger
The Prudent Investor's Guide to Hedge Funds by James P. Owen
Getting Started in Hedge Funds by Daniel A. Strachman
Hedge Funds The Courtesans of Capitalism by Peter Temple
Fundamentals of Hedge Fund Investing by William J. Crerend
The New Investment Superstars by Lois Peltz
Pioneering Portfolio Management by David F. Swensen
Searching for Alpha by Ben Warwick
All About Hedge Funds by Robert A. Jaeger
Investing in Hedge Funds by Joseph G. Nicolas
When Genius Failed:The Rise and Fall of Long-Term Capital Management by Roger Lowenstein

www.hedgeworld.com
www.hedgefund.net
www.vanhedge.com
www.cogenthedge.com
www.infovest21.com
www.thehfa.org
www.marhedge.com
www.canadianhedgewatch.com
www.albournevillage.com
www.hedgefundnews.com
www.hedgefundsreview.com
www.hedgefundcenter.com

For institutional book purchases of ten books or more, significant discounts apply. Please go to **www.hedgefundlady.com** for details or email **info@hedgefundlady.com**